D1506199

SPSS Tables™ 8.0

For more information about SPSS® software products, please visit our WWW site at *http://www.spss.com* or contact

Marketing Department
SPSS Inc.
444 North Michigan Avenue
Chicago, IL 60611
Tel: (312) 329-2400
Fax: (312) 329-3668

SPSS is a registered trademark and the other product names are the trademarks of SPSS Inc. for its proprietary computer software. No material describing such software may be produced or distributed without the written permission of the owners of the trademark and license rights in the software and the copyrights in the published materials.

The SOFTWARE and documentation are provided with RESTRICTED RIGHTS. Use, duplication, or disclosure by the Government is subject to restrictions as set forth in subdivision (c)(1)(ii) of The Rights in Technical Data and Computer Software clause at 52.227-7013. Contractor/manufacturer is SPSS Inc., 444 N. Michigan Avenue, Chicago, IL, 60611.

General notice: Other product names mentioned herein are used for identification purposes only and may be trademarks of their respective companies.

TableLook is a trademark of SPSS Inc.

SPSS Tables™ 8.0
Copyright © 1998 by SPSS Inc.
All rights reserved.
Printed in the United States of America.

No part of this publication may be reproduced, stored in a retrieval system, or transmitted, in any form or by any means, electronic, mechanical, photocopying, recording, or otherwise, without the prior written permission of the publisher.

 2 3 4 5 6 7 8 9 0   03 02 01 00 99 98

ISBN 1-56827-210-3

Preface

SPSS® 8.0 is a powerful software package for microcomputer data management and analysis. The Tables option is an add-on enhancement that enables you to prepare customized tables suitable for presentation or publication. The procedures in Tables must be used with the SPSS 8.0 Base and are completely integrated into that system.

The Tables option lets you combine large amounts of information in a single display. Through Tables you can access a wide variety of descriptive statistics.

Professionals in many different fields will find the Tables procedures beneficial. People in business, for example, can use Tables for periodic status reports and for analyses that support decision making. Market researchers and survey researchers can use Tables to meet the tabular style requirements of academic institutions or professional journals. The flexibility of Tables allows you to follow a prescribed style or, if you choose, design your own.

About This Manual

This manual is divided into three sections. The first section provides a guide to the various procedures available with the Tables option and describes how to obtain the appropriate tables with the dialog box interface. The second section gives an item-by-item description of each dialog box. The third section is a reference guide that provides complete syntax for all of the subcommands included in the Tables option. Most features of the system can be accessed through the dialog box interface, but some functionality can be accessed only through command syntax.

This manual contains two indexes: a subject index and a syntax index. The subject index covers the entire manual. The syntax index applies only to the syntax reference section.

Installation

To install Tables, follow the instructions for adding and removing features in the installation instructions supplied with the SPSS Base. (To start, double-click on the SPSS Setup icon.)

Compatibility

The SPSS system is designed to operate on many computer systems. See the installation instructions that came with your system for specific information on minimum and recommended requirements.

Serial Numbers

Your serial number is your identification number with SPSS Inc. You will need this serial number when you call SPSS Inc. for information regarding support, payment, or an upgraded system. The serial number was provided with your Base system. Before using the system, please copy this number to the registration card.

Customer Service

If you have any questions concerning your shipment or account, contact your local office, listed on page vi. Please have your serial number ready for identification when calling.

Training Seminars

SPSS Inc. provides both public and onsite training seminars for SPSS. All seminars feature hands-on workshops. SPSS seminars will be offered in major U.S. and European cities on a regular basis. For more information on these seminars, call your local office, listed on page vi.

Technical Support

The services of SPSS Technical Support are available to registered customers. Customers may contact Technical Support for assistance in using SPSS products or for installation help for one of the supported hardware environments. To reach Technical Support, see the SPSS home page on the World Wide Web at *http://www.spss.com*, or call your local office, listed on page vi. Be prepared to identify yourself, your organization, and the serial number of your system.

Tell Us Your Thoughts

Your comments are important. Please send us a letter and let us know about your experiences with SPSS products. We especially like to hear about new and interesting applications using the SPSS system. Write to SPSS Inc. Marketing Department, Attn: Director of Product Planning, 444 N. Michigan Avenue, Chicago, IL 60611.

Contacting SPSS

If you would like to be on our mailing list, contact one of our offices, listed on page vi, or visit our WWW site at *http://www.spss.com*. We will send you a copy of our newsletter and let you know about SPSS Inc. activities in your area.

SPSS Inc.
Chicago, Illinois, U.S.A.
Tel: 1.312.329.2400
Fax: 1.312.329.3668
Customer Service:
1.800.521.1337
Sales:
1.800.543.2185
sales@spss.com
Training:
1.800.543.6607
Technical Support:
1.312.329.3410
support@spss.com

SPSS Federal Systems
Arlington, Virginia, U.S.A.
Tel: 1.703.527.6777
Fax: 1.703.527.6866

SPSS Argentina srl
Buenos Aires, Argentina
Tel: +541.814.5030
Fax: +541.816.2616

SPSS Asia Pacific Pte. Ltd.
Singapore, Singapore
Tel: +65.2459.110
Fax: +65.2459.101

SPSS Australasia Pty. Ltd.
Sydney, Australia
Tel: +61.2.9954.5660
Fax: +61.2.9954.5616

SPSS Belgium
Heverlee, Belgium
Tel: +32.162.389.82
Fax: +32.1620.0888

SPSS Benelux BV
Gorinchem, The Netherlands
Tel: +31.183.636711
Fax: +31.183.635839

**SPSS Central and
Eastern Europe**
Woking, Surrey, U.K.
Tel: +44.(0)1483.719200
Fax: +44.(0)1483.719290

SPSS East Mediterranea and Africa
Herzlia, Israel
Tel: +972.9.526700
Fax: +972.9.526715

SPSS Finland Oy
Sinikalliontie, Finland
Tel: +358.9.524.801
Fax: +358.9.524.854

SPSS France SARL
Boulogne, France
Tel: +33.1.4699.9670
Fax: +33.1.4684.0180

SPSS Germany
Munich, Germany
Tel: +49.89.4890740
Fax: +49.89.4483115

SPSS Hellas SA
Athens, Greece
Tel: +30.1.7251925/7251950
Fax: +30.1.7249124

SPSS Hispanoportuguesa S.L.
Madrid, Spain
Tel: +34.91.447.3700
Fax: +34.91.448.6692

SPSS Ireland
Dublin, Ireland
Tel: +353.1.496.9007
Fax: +353.1.496.9008

SPSS Israel Ltd.
Herzlia, Israel
Tel: +972.9.526700
Fax: +972.9.526715

SPSS Italia srl
Bologna, Italy
Tel: +39.51.252573
Fax: +39.51.253285

SPSS Japan Inc.
Tokyo, Japan
Tel: +81.3.5466.5511
Fax: +81.3.5466.5621

SPSS Korea
Seoul, Korea
Tel: +82.2.3446.7651 3
Fax: +82.2.3446.7654

SPSS Latin America
Chicago, Illinois, U.S.A.
Tel: 1.312.494.3226
Fax: 1.312. 494.3227

SPSS Malaysia Sdn Bhd
Selangor, Malaysia
Tel: +603.704.5877
Fax: +603.704.5790

SPSS Mexico SA de CV
Mexico DF, Mexico
Tel: +52.5.575.3091
Fax: +52.5.575.2527

**SPSS Middle East and
South Asia**
Dubai, UAE
Tel: +91.80.227.7436/221.8962
Fax: +971.4.524669

SPSS Scandinavia AB
Stockholm, Sweden
Tel: +46.8.102610
Fax: +46.8.102550

SPSS Schweiz AG
Zurich, Switzerland
Tel: +41.1.201.0930
Fax: +41.1.201.0921

SPSS Singapore Pte. Ltd.
Singapore, Singapore
Tel: +065.5333190
Fax: +065.5334190

SPSS South Africa
Johannesburg, South Africa
Tel: +27.11.7067015
Fax: +27.11.7067091

SPSS Taiwan Corp.
Taipei, Republic of China
Tel: +886.2.5771100
Fax: +886.2.5701717

SPSS UK Ltd.
Woking, Surrey, U.K.
Tel: +44.1483.719200
Fax: +44.1483.719290

Contents

Syntax Reference

1 Overview

The SPSS Tables option includes four procedures:

- Basic Tables creates most simple tables. Basic Tables are described in Chapter 2 through Chapter 6.
- Tables of Frequencies creates compact frequency tables for multiple categorical variables that all have the same categories—such as ratings of several products on a 1-to-5 scale. See Chapter 7.
- Multiple Response Tables builds tables that use multiple response sets, such as those resulting from questions like "Which of the following names do you recognize?" Chapter 8 describes techniques for coding multiple response items and for using the Multiple Response Tables procedure.
- General Tables provides great flexibility for building complex tables with statistics, labels, and totals specified for each variable rather than for the table as a whole. It is described in Chapter 9 through Chapter 11. It can also include multiple response sets in its tables.

This chapter describes the main elements of a table and some of the terminology used in later chapters. Chapter 6 includes formatting options that apply to all types of tables.

Example Data File: The General Social Survey

The data file used in this manual is a portion of the 1991 General Social Survey (GSS). This survey has been conducted by the National Opinion Research Center from 1972 to the present. Many of the questions on the GSS duplicate questions on other surveys conducted between 1937 and 1978. For the complete General Social Survey or for questions regarding the survey, contact the Roper Center for Public Opinion Research, P.O. Box 440, Storrs, Connecticut 06268.

Variables

The way data are coded determines how they should be used in a table. A **categorical variable** can be used to define cells. Categorical variables usually have only a few possible values. Examples include variables that represent month, sex, department, and so on. Such variables subdivide the table into rows, columns, or layers, with one row, column, or layer for each unique value. In examining categorical variables, you are interested in the number or percentage of cases having a certain value (such as the number of females).

Summary variables can take on a wide range of values. Usually, the values of summary variables are cardinal numbers; that is, they record the quantity of something. For example, if three ages are recorded as 17, 39, and 68, they are recorded as values of a summary variable. If the same ages are recorded as young, middle-aged, and old, they are recorded as values of a category variable. Summary variables may be summarized with statistics such as the mean or standard deviation. For a description of how to use summary variables in tables, see Chapter 5 and Chapter 10.

A **multiple-response set** combines variables that are used to record multiple responses to a single item. For example, a respondent to a survey is asked an open-ended question or a question to which multiple responses can be given, such as, "List all of the problems you have had in the past 12 months." The respondent can list 1 problem or 8 or 10 problems. The responses are coded as multiple variables, which are treated as a single categorical variable in a table. For a description of how to code and use multiple-response variables, see Chapter 8.

Table Structure

Tables can have one, two, or three dimensions. Each dimension is defined by a single variable or a combination of variables. Variables that appear down the left side of a table are called **row variables**. They define the rows in a table. Variables that appear across the top of a table are called **column variables**. They define the columns in a table. Variables that appear in stacked tables are called **layer variables**. They define the third dimension of a table (see Figure 1.1).

Figure 1.1   Three physical dimensions of a table

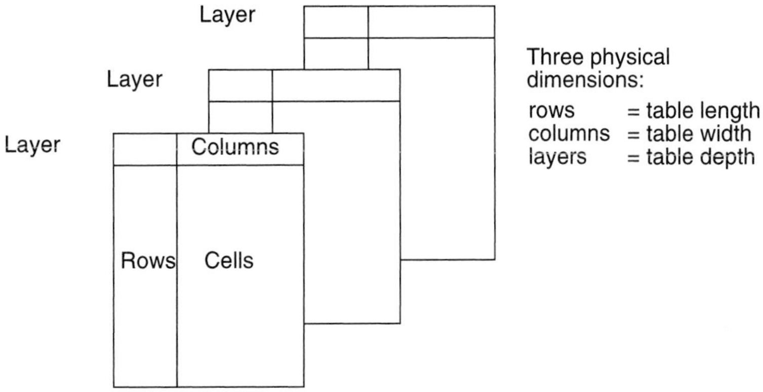

The body of a table is made up of **cells**, which contain the basic information conveyed by the table: counts, sums, means, percentages, and so on. A cell is formed by the intersection of a row and column of a table.

When multiple variables are placed in the same dimension, the display can be organized in two different ways. The variables can be **stacked** or **nested**. When variables are stacked, the categories are displayed separately, as though each variable is a separate table in the same display (see Figure 1.2).

Figure 1.2   Stacked variables

Other Variable and Answer are stacked in the row dimension

First Variable and Second Variable are stacked in the column dimension

		First Variable		Second Variable	
		A	B	Odd	Even
Other Variable	One	206	261	409	46
	Two	374	498	730	116
	Three	53	112	117	39
Answer	Yes	213	221	371	51
	No	200	305	413	69

When variables are nested, all categories of the nested variable are displayed for each category of the variable above it (see Figure 1.3).

Figure 1.3   Nested variables

Answer is nested under Other Variable in the rows

Second Variable is nested under First Variable in the columns

				First Variable			
				A		B	
				Second Variable		Second Variable	
				Odd	Even	Odd	Even
Other Variable	One	Answer	Yes	40	26	40	26
			No	9	18	31	15
				1			1
	Two	Answer	Yes	47	28	52	23
			No	69	36	90	53

The variable under which another variable is nested is called the **controlling variable**. For example, in Figure 1.3, *Other Variable* is the controlling variable for *Answer* in the rows.

You can rearrange the rows, columns, and layers after a table has been created in the Pivot Table Editor. To activate the Pivot Table Editor, double-click on the table in the Viewer. For more information about the Pivot Table Editor, see Chapter 6.

Using the Tables Dialog Boxes

Each of the table-building procedures listed under Custom Tables on the Statistics menu has its own main dialog box. Each of these contains buttons that open subdialog boxes. In general, a subdialog box has the same name as the button you push to open it.

In this manual, you will often be told to push a button in a particular dialog box. The name of the dialog box tells you how to open it. For example, if you are told to select **Across the top** under Statistics Labels in the Basic Tables Layout dialog box, you would select **Basic Tables** under Custom Tables on the Statistics menu. This opens the Basic Tables dialog box. You would click on **Layout** in the Basic Tables dialog box. This opens the Basic Tables Layout dialog box. Then you would select **Across the top** under Statistics Labels.

Selecting the Appropriate Procedure

Under most circumstances, you will want to use the Basic Tables procedure. The Basic Tables dialog box is easier to use than the General Tables dialog box, and it is capable of producing a wide variety of tables. All of the tools in the Basic Tables dialog box apply uniformly to all of the variables in the table it specifies. For example, if you select All combinations [nested] in the Basic Tables dialog box, all variables in all dimensions are nested beneath the previous variable in the same dimension, as shown in Figure 1.4.

Figure 1.4   Basic table

				Respondent's Sex					
				Male			Female		
				Race of Respondent			Race of Respondent		
				White	Black	Other	White	Black	Other
Region of the United States	North East	General Happiness	Very Happy	69	6	3	93	12	2
			Pretty Happy	160	14	2	201	30	5
			Not Too Happy	19	7		36	12	2
	South East	General Happiness	Very Happy	57	10	3	66	13	
			Pretty Happy	70	21	3	80	35	6
			Not Too Happy	10	2		21	12	2
	West	General Happiness	Very Happy	54	3	1	70	2	3
			Pretty Happy	96	3	5	123	13	5
			Not Too Happy	8	4	3	23	2	2

If you want to produce a table where nesting and stacking, statistics, or totals are applied differently to different variables, use the General Tables procedure. For example, the table in Figure 1.5 shows two variables nested in the rows, with two variables stacked in the columns.

Figure 1.5   General table

| | | | | Respondent's Sex | | Race of Respondent | | |
				Male	Female	White	Black	Other
Region of the United States	North East	General Happiness	Very Happy	78	107	162	18	5
			Pretty Happy	176	236	361	44	7
			Not Too Happy	26	50	55	19	2
	South East	General Happiness	Very Happy	70	79	123	23	3
			Pretty Happy	94	121	150	56	9
			Not Too Happy	12	35	31	14	2
	West	General Happiness	Very Happy	58	75	124	5	4
			Pretty Happy	104	141	219	16	10
			Not Too Happy	15	27	31	6	5

The Tables of Frequencies procedure produces special-purpose tables that show frequencies for category variables that each have the same categories. For example, the variables *obey*, *thnkself*, *popular*, *helpoth*, and *workhard* all have the categories *Most Important*, *2nd Important*, *3rd Important*, *4th Important*, and *Least Important*. The table of frequencies in Figure 1.6 shows frequencies for *obey*, *popular*, and *thnkself*.

Figure 1.6   Table of frequencies

	To Obey	To Be Well Liked or Popular	To Think for Oneself
	Count	Count	Count
Most Important	195	4	510
2nd Important	123	27	161
3rd Important	142	57	130
4th Important	343	185	135
Least Important	179	709	46

The Multiple Response Tables procedure provides a basic approach to tables that include multiple response sets. For example, Figure 1.7 shows the responses to the question "What problems have you experienced in the last 12 months?". Since many respondents indicated more than one type of problem (though some indicated none), the number of responses in the rows of this table come to more than the total number of respondents shown in the last row. You can also create multiple-response tables with the General Tables procedure if you need the additional flexibility that procedure provides.

Figure 1.7   Multiple Response Table

		Age Category					
		Under 30		30 to 50		Over 50	
		Count	Column %	Count	Column %	Count	Column %
Most Significant Problems in the Last 12 Months	Health	20	23%	48	33%	70	67%
	Finances	85	98%	91	63%	32	30%
	Family	12	14%	48	33%	16	15%
	Personal	13	15%	23	16%	5	5%
	Miscellaneous	21	24%	30	21%	29	28%
Total		**87**	**100%**	**144**	**100%**	**105**	**100%**

Pivoting Tables

Pivoting, or rotating, the elements of a table in the Pivot Table Editor adds functionality to the Tables option. Pivoting never changes the values in the cells; but by changing dimensions and hiding unnecessary columns, you can often obtain a table that presents the relationships in your data effectively without recreating the table itself. See Chapter 6 for a discussion of this feature.

Table Layout

The layout of a table is predetermined by the specified or default TableLook. Once a table is created, you can change its appearance using a variety of methods. These methods include modifications and/or application of a specific TableLook, online editing in the Pivot Table Editor, or pivoting a table. Establishing a default TableLook and applying, updating, or creating a new TableLook are the same in the Tables option as they are in the Base. See the *SPSS Base User's Guide* for a complete discussion of each function.

New in SPSS 8.0 is the ability to set maximum and minimum column widths to control when labels are wrapped. You can set these for an individual table or for a TableLook that you can apply repeatedly. They are discussed further in Chapter 6.

All of the tables illustrated in this book were created with the same TableLook. Once created, some of the tables were modified to present a better appearance. These modification included adjusting column widths and changing all totals to boldface type.

2 Basic Tables

In this chapter, you will learn how to create the three dimensions of a table using the Basic Tables procedure. You will also learn about the two methods of organizing multiple variables in the same dimension (nesting and stacking).

Specifying a Basic One-Dimensional Table

One of the GSS questions asks "Taken all together, how would you say things are these days—would you say that you are very happy, pretty happy, or not too happy?" A basic table can be constructed from the answers to this question. Figure 2.1 shows the variable *happy* in a table. Both the Basic Tables dialog box and the table it specifies are shown.

Figure 2.1   Simple one-dimensional table

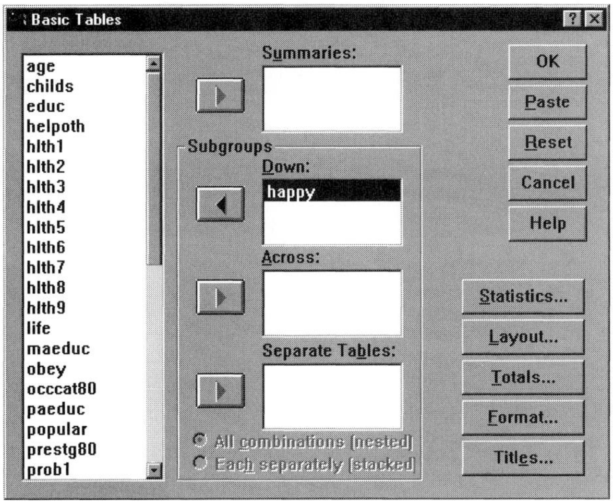

General Happiness	Very Happy	467
	Pretty Happy	872
	Not Too Happy	165

The table shown in Figure 2.1 begins with the title *General Happiness*, which is the label for the variable *happy*. If a variable doesn't have a label, the variable name is printed instead. The categories for the variable *happy* are shown with their respective value labels—*Very Happy*, *Pretty Happy*, and *Not Too Happy*. If a value has no label, the value is printed instead. The table in Figure 2.1 shows that most respondents are pretty happy.

Adding a Second Variable

Another related question on the GSS asks "In general, do you find life exciting, pretty routine, or dull?" The variable *life* can be stacked with *happy*, as shown in Figure 2.2. Notice in the dialog box that the button marked Each separately [stacked] is selected.

Figure 2.2   Two variables stacked in the same dimension

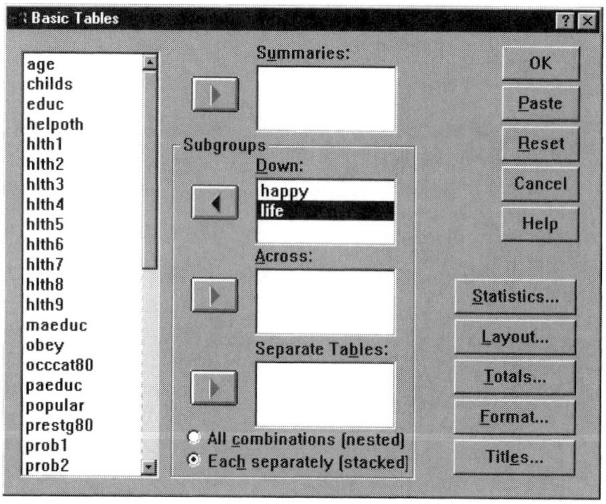

General Happiness	Very Happy	467
	Pretty Happy	872
	Not Too Happy	165
Is Life Exciting or Dull	Exciting	434
	Routine	505
	Dull	41

These two variables are **stacked** in a single dimension. When two variables are stacked, it is as though two separate tables are pasted one above the other. The first table is the same as the table in Figure 2.1. In the second table, you can see that most people find life either routine or exciting; very few people find life dull.

Adding a Second Dimension

A one-dimensional table gives basic information about how people in the survey feel, but it doesn't provide any information about the characteristics of those people. On the GSS, the variable *region* records the region of the United States in which the interview took place. In Figure 2.3, the variable *region* is added to the table. (*Note: Region* is recoded from the original GSS variable to produce more compact tables.) The table in Figure 2.3 shows *region* in the columns (Across under Subgroups), with *happy* and *life* stacked in the rows (Down under Subgroups). A table with category variables in the rows and columns is called a **crosstabulation**.

Figure 2.3   Adding a columns dimension—crosstabulation

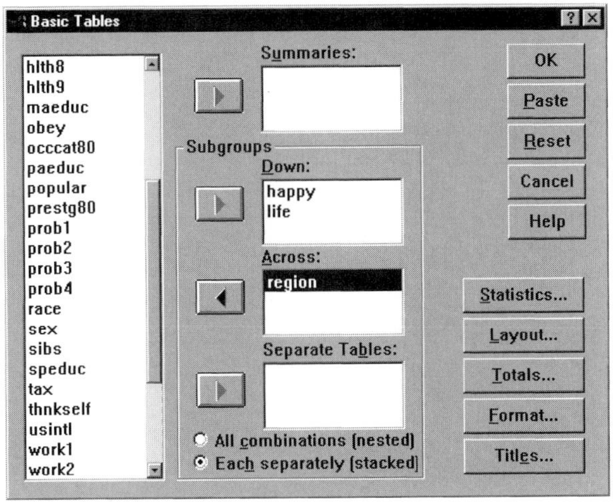

		Region of the United States		
		North East	South East	West
General Happiness	Very Happy	185	149	133
	Pretty Happy	412	215	245
	Not Too Happy	76	47	42
Is Life Exciting or Dull	Exciting	186	107	141
	Routine	228	148	129
	Dull	19	12	10

In Figure 2.3, there are 18 cells in the table, 3 for each of the 6 rows. The column heading is the label for the variable *region*. The value labels for *region* form the 3 columns.

This table allows you to see, in different regions, how happy people are and how exciting they find life. For example, you can see that most people in the Northeast are pretty happy and find life routine.

Adding a Third Dimension

Region of the country is only one characteristic of the respondents. Race and sex are also recorded on the GSS. How do people's outlooks differ, based on their race and sex? The table in Figure 2.4 shows *happy* and *life* stacked in the rows (Down under Subgroups), *race* in the columns (Across under Subgroups), and *sex* in the layers (Separate Tables under Subgroups). Layers are simply a way to display a three-dimensional table on a two-dimensional surface. To view the alternate layer, double-click on the table in the Viewer and then click the arrow on the layer pivot icon. A second table, with the alternate variable and value label, will replace the first table.

Figure 2.4   Adding a layer dimension

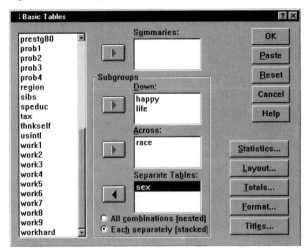

Respondent's Sex Male

		Race of Respondent		
		White	Black	Other
General Happiness	Very Happy	180	19	7
	Pretty Happy	326	38	10
	Not Too Happy	37	13	3
Is Life Exciting or Dull	Exciting	181	25	7
	Routine	173	20	7
	Dull	11	1	

Respondent's Sex Female

		Race of Respondent		
		White	Black	Other
General Happiness	Very Happy	229	27	5
	Pretty Happy	404	78	16
	Not Too Happy	80	26	6
Is Life Exciting or Dull	Exciting	190	26	5
	Routine	240	49	16
	Dull	23	5	1

From the table in Figure 2.4, you can see that more women find life routine while more men find life exciting.

Nesting Variables

Nesting is a method of displaying a multiway crosstabulation in a single dimension. To illustrate nesting, we need to start with a simpler table. Figure 2.5 shows a table with *happy* in the rows, *race* in the columns, and *sex* in the layers.

Figure 2.5   One variable in each dimension

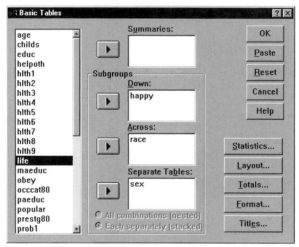

Respondent's Sex Male

		Race of Respondent		
		White	Black	Other
General Happiness	Very Happy	180	19	7
	Pretty Happy	326	38	10
	Not Too Happy	37	13	3

Respondent's Sex Female

		Race of Respondent		
		White	Black	Other
General Happiness	Very Happy	229	27	5
	Pretty Happy	404	78	16
	Not Too Happy	80	26	6

This table is the same as the table in Figure 2.4, except that the variable *life* is no longer in the rows. (*Note*: To view the alternate layer, double-click on the table in the Viewer and then use the drop-down list that appears at the dimension label to select the layer you want to see.) There is now one variable in each dimension. To display the same information in two dimensions, nest *race* under *sex* in the columns, as shown in Figure 2.6. Notice that All combinations [nested], rather than Each separately [stacked], is selected. You can see that the numbers are the same, as though there were three dimensions (see Figure 2.5). However, in Figure 2.6, there are only two dimensions. Under each category of *sex*, there is a column for each category of *race*.

Figure 2.6   Nested column variable

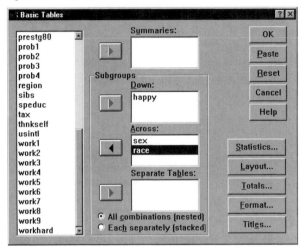

	Male			Female		
	White	Black	Other	White	Black	Other
Very Happy	180	19	7	229	27	5
Pretty Happy	326	38	10	404	78	16
Not Too Happy	37	13	3	80	26	6

If you want to put all three variables in the rows, stack *sex*, *race*, and *happy* in the rows, as shown in Figure 2.7. As long as All combinations [nested] is selected, each variable on the Subgroups list is nested under the previous variable on the same list. The information is the same as that in the three-dimensional table in Figure 2.5 and the two-dimensional table in Figure 2.6, except that there is only one dimension. You can also use the Pivot Table Editor to reduce the dimensions of a table—in this case by moving the layer icon into the column. Creating the table initially with more dimensions rather than with nesting gives you more display options with the Pivot Table Editor because you cannot break apart a dimension created by two or more multiple variables.

Figure 2.7   Two levels of nesting in the rows

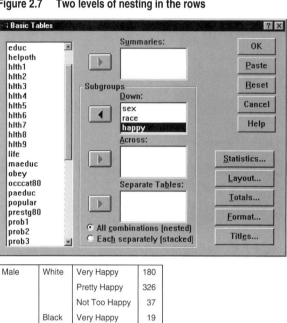

Male	White	Very Happy	180
		Pretty Happy	326
		Not Too Happy	37
	Black	Very Happy	19
		Pretty Happy	38
		Not Too Happy	13
	Other	Very Happy	7
		Pretty Happy	10
		Not Too Happy	3
Female	White	Very Happy	229
		Pretty Happy	404
		Not Too Happy	80
	Black	Very Happy	27
		Pretty Happy	78
		Not Too Happy	26
	Other	Very Happy	5
		Pretty Happy	16
		Not Too Happy	6

To improve the look of the two previous tables, Label groups with value labels only was selected in the Basic Tables Layout dialog box. You can also hide rows and/or columns in the Pivot Table Editor for the same effect. For a complete discussion of table format options, see Chapter 6.

Deciding Which Variable Goes in Which Dimension

Although there are no hard and fast rules, there are some conventions that can help you decide which variables should appear in which table dimension. Survey researchers generally use the terms independent and dependent variables. Variation in an **independent variable** logically precedes, somehow predicts, or even causes variation in the **dependent variable**. For example, the sex of an individual clearly precedes the individual's opinion. (The individual's sex might influence the opinion, but the opinion can't affect the individual's sex.) Market researchers have the same basic view of variables, except that for them, causality is not nearly as important as prediction. For example, a market researcher would be interested in predicting how women react to various advertising schemes if women are the target group for an advertising campaign.

The dominant convention for both survey and market researchers is to present the dependent variables in rows and the independent variables in columns and layers. If nesting is used, the convention is to nest the dependent variables under the independent variables.

3 Percentages in Basic Tables

Requesting the right statistics in a table can greatly simplify its interpretation. While counts within the cells are the most basic information you need, percentages transform counts into measures that are more easily compared.

This chapter explores how to specify percentages, how to get them to add to 100% in the direction that you want, and how to place the statistics labels in the proper dimension.

Requesting Column Percentages

In Chapter 2, the tables show the number of respondents who are happy and who find life exciting. In a table of opinions, one of the first questions people ask is "What proportion of the respondents in each category holds each opinion?"

The tables in Chapter 2 used counts. The table in Figure 3.1 shows *happy* and *life* by *race* and *sex* with counts only.

Figure 3.1   Basic table with counts only

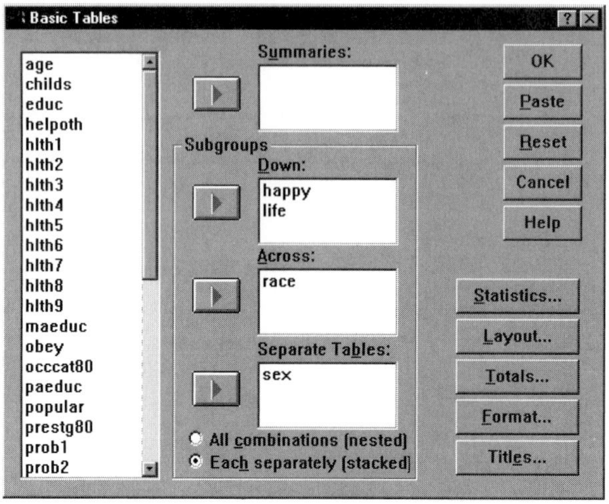

Respondent's Sex Male

		Race of Respondent		
		White	Black	Other
General Happiness	Very Happy	180	19	7
	Pretty Happy	326	38	10
	Not Too Happy	37	13	3
Is Life Exciting or Dull	Exciting	181	25	7
	Routine	173	20	7
	Dull	11	1	

Respondent's Sex Female

		Race of Respondent		
		White	Black	Other
General Happiness	Very Happy	229	27	5
	Pretty Happy	404	78	16
	Not Too Happy	80	26	6
Is Life Exciting or Dull	Exciting	190	26	5
	Routine	240	49	16
	Dull	23	5	1

An easier way to evaluate proportions is to display percentages in a table. It would be nice to be able to read down each column to see what percentage of each category is very happy, somewhat happy, or not too happy. The statistic that shows this is the column percentage. The table in Figure 3.2 shows both counts and column percentages.

Figure 3.2   Basic table with counts and column percentages

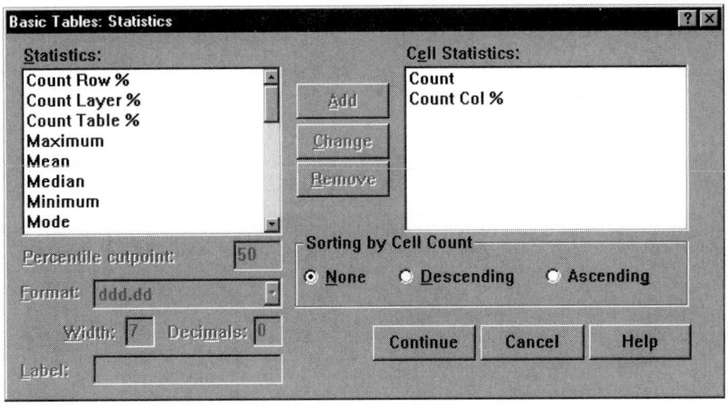

Respondent's Sex Male

		Race of Respondent					
		White		Black		Other	
		Count	Col %	Count	Col %	Count	Col %
General Happiness	Very Happy	180	33.1%	19	27.1%	7	35.0%
	Pretty Happy	326	60.0%	38	54.3%	10	50.0%
	Not Too Happy	37	6.8%	13	18.6%	3	15.0%
Is Life Exciting or Dull	Exciting	181	49.6%	25	54.3%	7	50.0%
	Routine	173	47.4%	20	43.5%	7	50.0%
	Dull	11	3.0%	1	2.2%		

Respondent's Sex Female

		Race of Respondent					
		White		Black		Other	
		Count	Col %	Count	Col %	Count	Col %
General Happiness	Very Happy	229	32.1%	27	20.6%	5	18.5%
	Pretty Happy	404	56.7%	78	59.5%	16	59.3%
	Not Too Happy	80	11.2%	26	19.8%	6	22.2%
Is Life Exciting or Dull	Exciting	190	41.9%	26	32.5%	5	22.7%
	Routine	240	53.0%	49	61.3%	16	72.7%
	Dull	23	5.1%	5	6.3%	1	4.5%

Beneath each category of *race*, there is a column with counts and a column with percentages. Because the selected percentage was column percentages, each category of *race* (each column) adds up to 100% within each opinion variable (*happy* and *life*).

You can see that, overall, male respondents are more likely to be happy than female respondents, white respondents are more likely to be happy than black respondents, and black male respondents are more likely to find life exciting than female or white male respondents.

Eliminating Decimal Places

Effective interpretation of percentages often requires only whole number percentages. To eliminate the decimal position, select the percentage on the Cell Statistics list (Count Col %) and change 1 to 0 in the Decimals text box. This produces the table shown in Figure 3.3.

Figure 3.3   Column percentages with no decimal

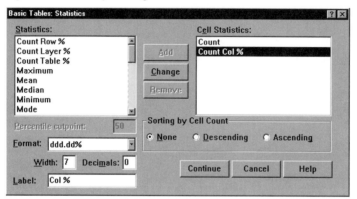

Respondent's Sex Male

		Race of Respondent					
		White		Black		Other	
		Count	Col %	Count	Col %	Count	Col %
General Happiness	Very Happy	180	33%	19	27%	7	35%
	Pretty Happy	326	60%	38	54%	10	50%
	Not Too Happy	37	7%	13	19%	3	15%
Is Life Exciting or Dull	Exciting	181	50%	25	54%	7	50%
	Routine	173	47%	20	43%	7	50%
	Dull	11	3%	1	2%		

Respondent's Sex Female

		Race of Respondent					
		White		Black		Other	
		Count	Col %	Count	Col %	Count	Col %
General Happiness	Very Happy	229	32%	27	21%	5	19%
	Pretty Happy	404	57%	78	60%	16	59%
	Not Too Happy	80	11%	26	20%	6	22%
Is Life Exciting or Dull	Exciting	190	42%	26	33%	5	23%
	Routine	240	53%	49	61%	16	73%
	Dull	23	5%	5	6%	1	5%

You can also change the number of decimal places displayed after the table is created in the Pivot Table Editor.

To change the number of decimal places in a table after it is created, select the data to be updated and from the Pivot Table menus choose:

Format
  Cell Properties...

This opens the Cell Properties dialog box, as shown in Figure 3.4.

Figure 3.4   Cell Properties Value tab

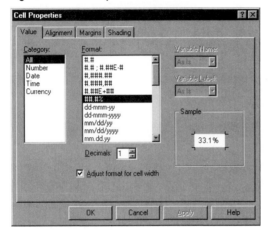

Either scroll to the desired number of decimal places or enter the number in the Decimals text box on the Value tab. Click on **OK**. The decimal places in the selected data will be updated. For a complete discussion of the Cell Properties dialog box, see the *SPSS Base User's Guide*.

Percentages with Nesting

In the last two examples, the variable *life* was stacked under the variable *happy*. It might be interesting to see the interaction of happiness and excitement for each sex. The table in Figure 3.5 shows *life* nested under *happy* in the rows and *sex* in the columns.

Figure 3.5   Column percentages with nesting

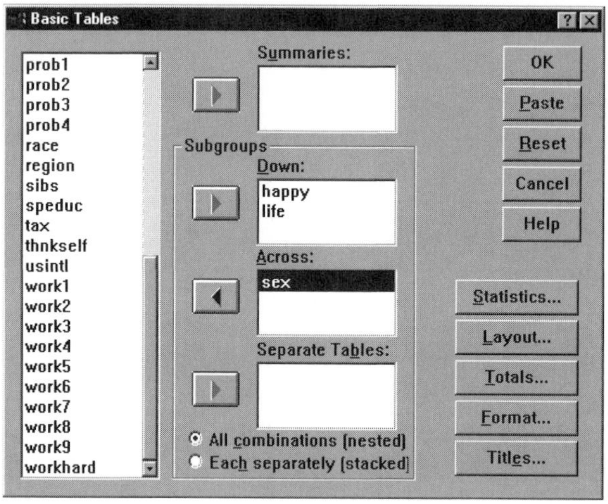

				Respondent's Sex			
				Male		Female	
				Count	Col %	Count	Col %
General Happiness	Very Happy	Is Life Exciting or Dull	Exciting	95	23%	100	18%
			Routine	37	9%	61	11%
			Dull	1	0%	1	0%
	Pretty Happy	Is Life Exciting or Dull	Exciting	105	25%	113	21%
			Routine	144	34%	194	35%
			Dull	4	1%	8	1%
	Not Too Happy	Is Life Exciting or Dull	Exciting	13	3%	8	1%
			Routine	17	4%	44	8%
			Dull	6	1%	20	4%

Since *happy* and *life* are now nested, each sex adds up to 100% over the whole column. Here you can see that the distribution of opinions is similar between males and females. The largest group of people is pretty happy and finds life routine. The smallest group of people is very happy and finds life dull.

Requesting Row Percentages

We will now focus on the interaction between happiness and excitement about life. The table in Figure 3.6 shows *happy* in the rows and *life* in the columns. The column percentages in this table show the percentage of respondents in each excitement category who are very happy, pretty happy, or not too happy.

Figure 3.6   Column percentages with happy by life

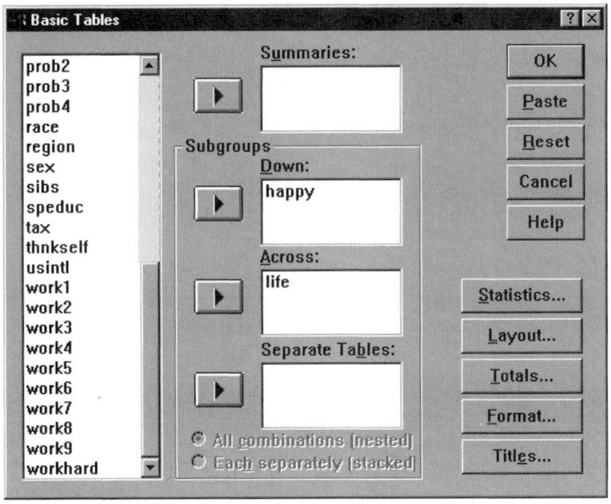

		Is Life Exciting or Dull					
		Exciting		Routine		Dull	
		Count	Col %	Count	Col %	Count	Col %
General Happiness	Very Happy	195	45%	98	20%	2	5%
	Pretty Happy	218	50%	338	68%	12	30%
	Not Too Happy	21	5%	61	12%	26	65%

Of those who find life exciting, 45% are very happy and 50% are pretty happy. Of those who find life routine, 68% are pretty happy. Of those who find life dull, 65% are not too happy.

To look at the percentage of respondents in each happiness category who find life exciting, routine, or dull, you can switch *life* and *happy* in the table or you can change the kind of percentage. Instead of column percentages, you can now look at row percentages. The table in Figure 3.7 shows counts and row percentages. The percentages add up to 100% across each row.

Figure 3.7   Counts and row percentages

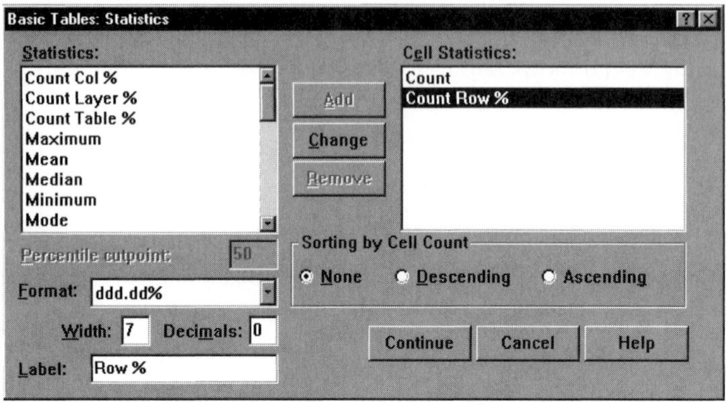

		Is Life Exciting or Dull					
		Exciting		Routine		Dull	
		Count	Row %	Count	Row %	Count	Row %
General Happiness	Very Happy	195	66%	98	33%	2	1%
	Pretty Happy	218	38%	338	60%	12	2%
	Not Too Happy	21	19%	61	56%	26	24%

Of those people who are very happy, 66% find life exciting. Of those who are pretty happy, 60% find life routine. Of those who are not too happy, 56% find life routine.

Selecting Different Statistics Labels Dimensions

In the last table, the percentages are row percentages, but the statistics labels appear in the columns. To change the statistics labels dimension to the rows, select Down the left side under Statistics Labels in the Basic Tables Layout dialog box. This produces the table shown in Figure 3.8.

Figure 3.8   Statistics labels in the rows dimension

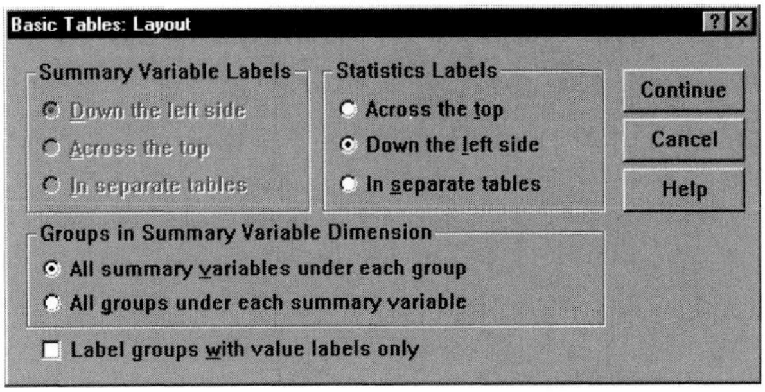

| | | | Is Life Exciting or Dull | | |
			Exciting	Routine	Dull
General Happiness	Very Happy	Count	195	98	2
		Row %	66%	33%	1%
	Pretty Happy	Count	218	338	12
		Row %	38%	60%	2%
	Not Too Happy	Count	21	61	26
		Row %	19%	56%	24%

The statistics in this table are the same as those in Figure 3.7. Instead of a column for counts and a column for percentages under each category for *life*, there is a row for counts and a row for percentages under each category for *happy*.

Layer Percentages

You have already seen a breakdown of *happy* by *life* by *sex* in the nested table shown in Figure 3.5. If you want to emphasize the relationship between happiness and excitement about life within each sex separately, move *sex* into Separate Tables under Subgroups. Now *happy* is in the rows dimension, *life* is in the columns dimension, and *sex* is in the layers dimension. The table is shown in Figure 3.9 with counts only.

Note: Reset the dialog box before selecting criteria for this table.

Figure 3.9   Happy by life by sex with counts only

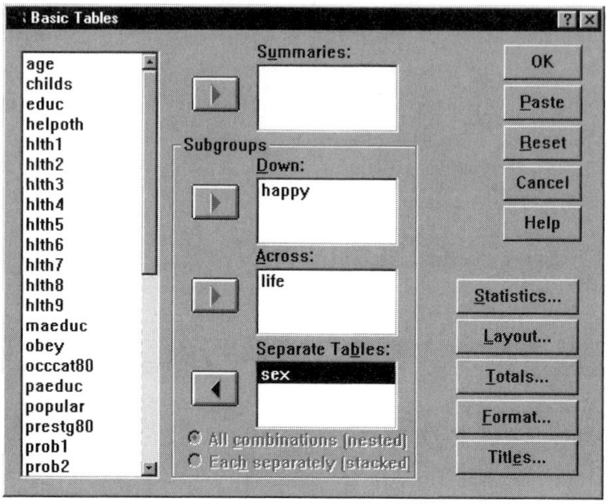

Respondent's Sex Male

		Is Life Exciting or Dull		
		Exciting	Routine	Dull
General Happiness	Very Happy	95	37	1
	Pretty Happy	105	144	4
	Not Too Happy	13	17	6

Respondent's Sex Female

		Is Life Exciting or Dull		
		Exciting	Routine	Dull
General Happiness	Very Happy	100	61	1
	Pretty Happy	113	194	8
	Not Too Happy	8	44	20

To force all of the responses for each sex to add up to 100%, choose Count Layer % in the Basic Tables Statistics dialog box. The resulting table with counts and layer percentages is shown in Figure 3.10.

Figure 3.10   Counts and layer percentages

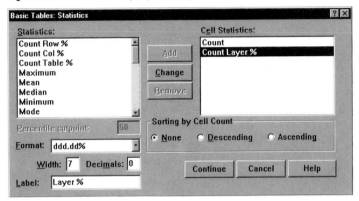

Respondent's Sex Male

			Is Life Exciting or Dull		
			Exciting	Routine	Dull
General Happiness	Very Happy	Count	95	37	1
		Layer %	23%	9%	0%
	Pretty Happy	Count	105	144	4
		Layer %	25%	34%	1%
	Not Too Happy	Count	13	17	6
		Layer %	3%	4%	1%

Respondent's Sex Female

			Is Life Exciting or Dull		
			Exciting	Routine	Dull
General Happiness	Very Happy	Count	100	61	1
		Layer %	18%	11%	0%
	Pretty Happy	Count	113	194	8
		Layer %	21%	35%	1%
	Not Too Happy	Count	8	44	20
		Layer %	1%	8%	4%

The statistics are the same as those in Figure 3.5, but the organization of the table is completely different. Instead of nesting *happy* and *life* together in the rows, *happy* is in the rows and *life* is in the columns. *Sex* is moved from the columns to the layers, and the selected statistic is layer percentages rather than column percentages.

Note: To create the table shown in Figure 3.10, you must select Down the left side under Statistics Labels in the Basic Tables Layout dialog box.

4 Totals in Basic Tables

Totals allow you to summarize the values represented in more than one cell. This chapter describes totals for counts and percentages in the Basic Tables procedure. Later chapters describe totals for other statistics and how to get totals for a General Tables or a Tables of Frequencies procedure.

Group Totals

When you want a total for a simple table, you can use group totals. For example, Figure 4.1 shows a three-dimensional table from Chapter 3.

Figure 4.1   Simple three-dimensional table with counts and column percentages

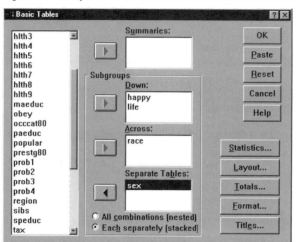

Respondent's Sex Male

		Race of Respondent					
		White		Black		Other	
		Count	Col %	Count	Col %	Count	Col %
General Happiness	Very Happy	180	33.1%	19	27.1%	7	35.0%
	Pretty Happy	326	60.0%	38	54.3%	10	50.0%
	Not Too Happy	37	6.8%	13	18.6%	3	15.0%
Is Life Exciting or Dull	Exciting	181	49.6%	25	54.3%	7	50.0%
	Routine	173	47.4%	20	43.5%	7	50.0%
	Dull	11	3.0%	1	2.2%		

Respondent's Sex Female

		Race of Respondent					
		White		Black		Other	
		Count	Col %	Count	Col %	Count	Col %
General Happiness	Very Happy	229	32.1%	27	20.6%	5	18.5%
	Pretty Happy	404	56.7%	78	59.5%	16	59.3%
	Not Too Happy	80	11.2%	26	19.8%	6	22.2%
Is Life Exciting or Dull	Exciting	190	41.9%	26	32.5%	5	22.7%
	Routine	240	53.0%	49	61.3%	16	72.7%
	Dull	23	5.1%	5	6.3%	1	4.5%

Happy and *life* are stacked in the rows. *Race* is in the columns, and *sex* is in the layers. Figure 4.2 shows the same table with group totals. To produce this table, click on Totals to open the Basic Tables Totals dialog box, and select Totals over each group variable.

Figure 4.2   Simple three-dimensional table with group totals

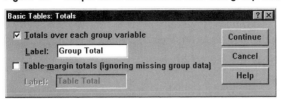

Respondent's Sex Male

		Race of Respondent						Group Total	
		White		Black		Other			
		Count	Col %	Count	Col %	Count	Col %	Count	Col %
General Happiness	Very Happy	180	33.1%	19	27.1%	7	35.0%	206	32.5%
	Pretty Happy	326	60.0%	38	54.3%	10	50.0%	374	59.1%
	Not Too Happy	37	6.8%	13	18.6%	3	15.0%	53	8.4%
Group Total		**543**	**100.0%**	**70**	**100.0%**	**20**	**100.0%**	**633**	**100.0%**
Is Life Exciting or Dull	Exciting	181	49.6%	25	54.3%	7	50.0%	213	50.1%
	Routine	173	47.4%	20	43.5%	7	50.0%	200	47.1%
	Dull	11	3.0%	1	2.2%			12	2.8%
Group Total		**365**	**100.0%**	**46**	**100.0%**	**14**	**100.0%**	**425**	**100.0%**

Respondent's Sex Female

		Race of Respondent						Group Total	
		White		Black		Other			
		Count	Col %	Count	Col %	Count	Col %	Count	Col %
General Happiness	Very Happy	229	32.1%	27	20.6%	5	18.5%	261	30.0%
	Pretty Happy	404	56.7%	78	59.5%	16	59.3%	498	57.2%
	Not Too Happy	80	11.2%	26	19.8%	6	22.2%	112	12.9%
Group Total		**713**	**100.0%**	**131**	**100.0%**	**27**	**100.0%**	**871**	**100.0%**
Is Life Exciting or Dull	Exciting	190	41.9%	26	32.5%	5	22.7%	221	39.8%
	Routine	240	53.0%	49	61.3%	16	72.7%	305	55.0%
	Dull	23	5.1%	5	6.3%	1	4.5%	29	5.2%
Group Total		**453**	**100.0%**	**80**	**100.0%**	**22**	**100.0%**	**555**	**100.0%**

Group Total

		Race of Respondent						Group Total	
		White		Black		Other			
		Count	Col %	Count	Col %	Count	Col %	Count	Col %
General Happiness	Very Happy	409	32.6%	46	22.9%	12	25.5%	467	31.1%
	Pretty Happy	730	58.1%	116	57.7%	26	55.3%	872	58.0%
	Not Too Happy	117	9.3%	39	19.4%	9	19.1%	165	11.0%
Group Total		**1256**	**100.0%**	**201**	**100.0%**	**47**	**100.0%**	**1504**	**100.0%**
Is Life Exciting or Dull	Exciting	371	45.4%	51	40.5%	12	33.3%	434	44.3%
	Routine	413	50.5%	69	54.8%	23	63.9%	505	51.5%
	Dull	34	4.2%	6	4.8%	1	2.8%	41	4.2%
Group Total		**818**	**100.0%**	**126**	**100.0%**	**36**	**100.0%**	**980**	**100.0%**

Stacked variables can be thought of as separate tables pasted together. Each stacked variable shows all of the nonmissing cases in the data. Thus, each stacked variable adds up to 100%.

Notice that when variables are stacked, there is a total for each variable. The totals share the same statistics as the rest of the table.

Group Totals of Nested Variables

Figure 4.3 shows a two-dimensional table with group totals. *Happy* and *life* are nested in the rows and *race* is in the columns.

Figure 4.3　　Group totals for a nested variable

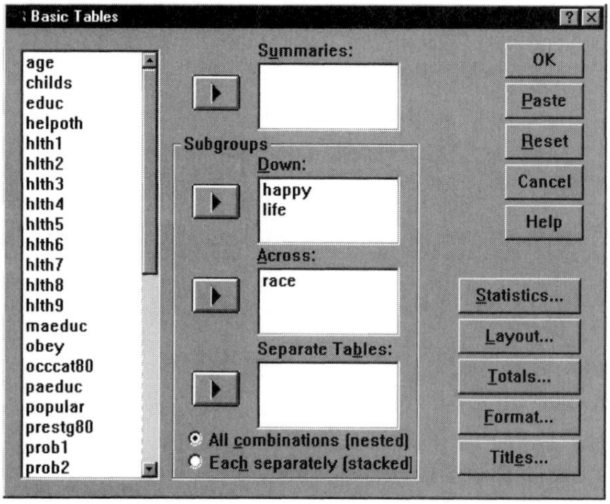

				White Count	White Col %	Black Count	Black Col %	Other Count	Other Col %	Group Total Count	Group Total Col %
General Happiness	Very Happy	Is Life Exciting or Dull	Exciting	172	21.2%	18	14.4%	5	14.3%	195	20.1%
			Routine	84	10.4%	11	8.8%	3	8.6%	98	10.1%
			Dull	1	.1%	1	.8%			2	.2%
		Group Total		257	31.7%	30	24.0%	8	22.9%	295	30.4%
	Pretty Happy	Is Life Exciting or Dull	Exciting	188	23.2%	24	19.2%	6	17.1%	218	22.5%
			Routine	279	34.4%	45	36.0%	14	40.0%	338	34.8%
			Dull	12	1.5%					12	1.2%
		Group Total		479	59.1%	69	55.2%	20	57.1%	568	58.5%
	Not Too Happy	Is Life Exciting or Dull	Exciting	11	1.4%	9	7.2%	1	2.9%	21	2.2%
			Routine	44	5.4%	12	9.6%	5	14.3%	61	6.3%
			Dull	20	2.5%	5	4.0%	1	2.9%	26	2.7%
		Group Total		75	9.2%	26	20.8%	7	20.0%	108	11.1%

Note: Columns are grouped under "Race of Respondent" (White, Black, Other) and "Group Total".

Here *life* is nested under *happy*. A total for *life* is reported within each category of *happy*. Each group total for *life* is less than 100%, but together the group totals for *life* add up to 100% in each column. Since there is no layer variable, there is no layer total.

Table Totals

Table totals are not like group totals. Group totals will total only values shown in the table. They will not count user-missing or system-missing values. Table totals, on the other hand, will. For example, Figure 4.4 shows a table with group and table totals. *Happy* and *life* are stacked in the rows and *sex* is in the columns.

Figure 4.4   Table totals for a stacked variable

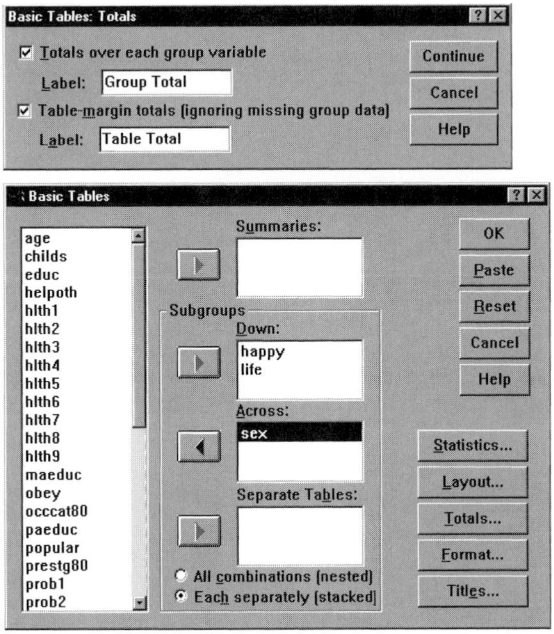

		Respondent's Sex				Group Total		Table Total	
		Male		Female					
		Count	Col %	Count	Col %	Count	Col %	Count	Col %
General Happiness	Very Happy	206	32.5%	261	30.0%	467	31.1%	467	31.1%
	Pretty Happy	374	59.1%	498	57.2%	872	58.0%	872	58.0%
	Not Too Happy	53	8.4%	112	12.9%	165	11.0%	165	11.0%
Group Total		**633**	**100.0%**	**871**	**100.0%**	**1504**	**100.0%**	**1504**	**100.0%**
Is Life Exciting or Dull	Exciting	213	50.1%	221	39.8%	434	44.3%	434	44.3%
	Routine	200	47.1%	305	55.0%	505	51.5%	505	51.5%
	Dull	12	2.8%	29	5.2%	41	4.2%	41	4.2%
Group Total		**425**	**100.0%**	**555**	**100.0%**	**980**	**100.0%**	**980**	**100.0%**
Table Total		**636**	**100.0%**	**881**	**100.0%**	**1517**	**100.0%**	**1517**	**100.0%**

The group totals for *happy* are larger than the group totals for *life* because more people didn't answer the "life" question (there are more missing values). The table totals at the bottom of each column are larger than either group total because the table total counts all values, whether or not they are missing.

The group and table totals in each row are the same because the interviewer was able to determine the sex of all of the respondents (there are no missing values for *sex*). If there are no missing data, table totals will generally take less space in a table.

Table Totals of Nested Variables

Figure 4.5 shows a table with *life* nested under *happy* in the rows and *sex* in the columns. Both group and table totals are shown. While group totals show the total within each category of *happy*, table totals show the total across the whole table.

Figure 4.5   Table totals for a nested variable

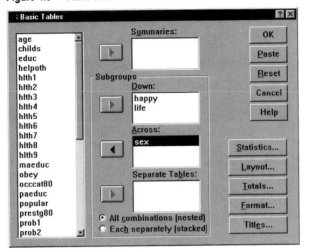

				Respondent's Sex				Group Total		Table Total	
				Male		Female					
				Count	Col %	Count	Col %	Count	Col %	Count	Col %
General Happiness	Very Happy	Is Life Exciting or Dull	Exciting	95	22.5%	100	18.2%	195	20.1%	195	20.1%
			Routine	37	8.8%	61	11.1%	98	10.1%	98	10.1%
			Dull	1	.2%	1	.2%	2	.2%	2	.2%
		Group Total		133	31.5%	162	29.5%	295	30.4%	295	30.4%
	Pretty Happy	Is Life Exciting or Dull	Exciting	105	24.9%	113	20.6%	218	22.5%	218	22.5%
			Routine	144	34.1%	194	35.3%	338	34.8%	338	34.8%
			Dull	4	.9%	8	1.5%	12	1.2%	12	1.2%
		Group Total		253	60.0%	315	57.4%	568	58.5%	568	58.5%
	Not Too Happy	Is Life Exciting or Dull	Exciting	13	3.1%	8	1.5%	21	2.2%	21	2.2%
			Routine	17	4.0%	44	8.0%	61	6.3%	61	6.3%
			Dull	6	1.4%	20	3.6%	26	2.7%	26	2.7%
		Group Total		36	8.5%	72	13.1%	108	11.1%	108	11.1%
Table Total				636	100.0%	881	100.0%	1517	100.0%	1517	100.0%

Sorting Cells

Suppose you want to rearrange the cells of a table, organizing it based on the counts in the cells. You can arrange the categories in either ascending or descending order. For example, the table shown in Figure 4.6 is unsorted.

Figure 4.6   Unsorted table

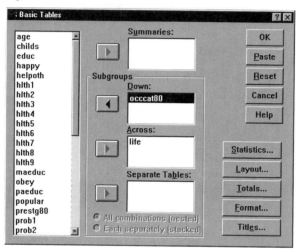

		Is Life Exciting or Dull						Group Total	
		Exciting		Routine		Dull			
		Count	Col %	Count	Col %	Count	Col %	**Count**	**Col %**
Occupational Category	Managerial and Professional Specialty	129	31.5%	78	16.8%	3	8.6%	**210**	**23.1%**
	Technical, Sales, and Administrative Support	125	30.6%	156	33.6%	13	37.1%	**294**	**32.4%**
	Service	56	13.7%	73	15.7%	6	17.1%	**135**	**14.9%**
	Farming, Forest, and Fishing	16	3.9%	9	1.9%			**25**	**2.8%**
	Precision Production, Craft, and Repair	38	9.3%	65	14.0%	6	17.1%	**109**	**12.0%**
	Operation, Fabrication, and General Labor	45	11.0%	83	17.9%	7	20.0%	**135**	**14.9%**
Group Total		**409**	**100.0%**	**464**	**100.0%**	**35**	**100.0%**	**908**	**100.0%**

To sort the table in descending order, click on Statistics to open the Basic Tables Statistics dialog box. Select Descending under Sorting by Cell Count. The table shown in Figure 4.7 is sorted in descending order.

Figure 4.7   Table sorted in descending order

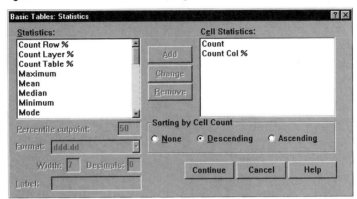

| | | Is Life Exciting or Dull | | | | | | Group Total | |
| | | Routine | | Exciting | | Dull | | | |
		Count	Col %	Count	Col %	Count	Col %	Count	Col %
Occupational Category	Technical, Sales, and Administrative Support	156	33.6%	125	30.6%	13	37.1%	294	32.4%
	Managerial and Professional Specialty	78	16.8%	129	31.5%	3	8.6%	210	23.1%
	Service	73	15.7%	56	13.7%	6	17.1%	135	14.9%
	Operation, Fabrication, and General Labor	83	17.9%	45	11.0%	7	20.0%	135	14.9%
	Precision Production, Craft, and Repair	65	14.0%	38	9.3%	6	17.1%	109	12.0%
	Farming, Forest, and Fishing	9	1.9%	16	3.9%			25	2.8%
Group Total		464	100.0%	409	100.0%	35	100.0%	908	100.0%

All categories in the table are sorted. The order is always determined by counts, regardless of what statistics are selected. Notice that the counts for both the total column and the total row are in descending order.

5 Means and Other Summary Statistics in Basic Tables

Statistics such as the mean, standard deviation, and range are used to summarize non-categorical variables, such as temperature, height, or distance. Summary statistics can be displayed alone or broken down into subcategories.

Summarizing Variables

Unless a variable such as age, years of education, or number of siblings is coded as a small number of categories, you usually want a summary, such as an average, for that variable. To summarize the variable, move it from the source variables list to the Summaries list. By default, the mean of a summary variable is shown in the table.

On the GSS, there are a number of summary variables, which include the age and education of the respondent. To create a table with summary variables, simply add them to the Summaries list and click on OK. Figure 5.1 shows a table with the mean age, education, father's education, mother's education, spouse's education, number of children, and siblings.

Figure 5.1   Mean of multiple variables

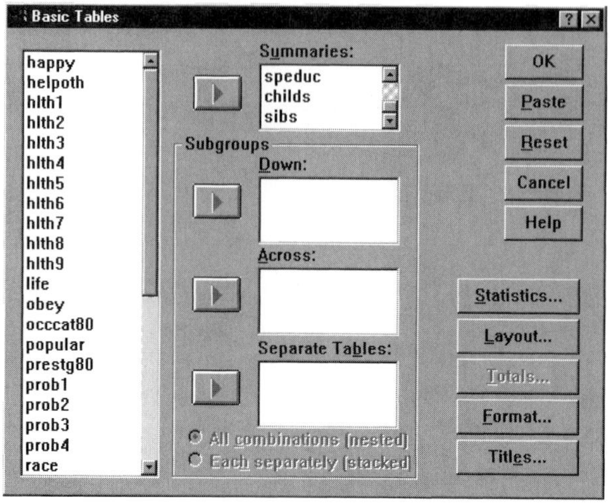

Age of Respondent	46
Highest Year of School Completed	13
Highest Year School Completed, Father	11
Highest Year School Completed, Mother	11
Highest Year School Completed, Spouse	13
Number of Children	2
Number of Brothers and Sisters	4

You can show more than one statistic for a summary variable by moving Mean, Range, and Std Deviation to the Cell Statistics list in the Basic Tables Statistics dialog box. Click on Continue to generate the table shown in Figure 5.2.

Figure 5.2   Multiple summary statistics

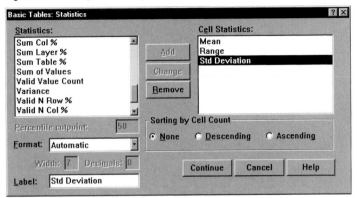

	Mean	Range	Std Deviation
Age of Respondent	46	71	18
Highest Year of School Completed	13	20	3
Highest Year School Completed, Father	11	20	4
Highest Year School Completed, Mother	11	20	3
Highest Year School Completed, Spouse	13	20	3
Number of Children	2	8	2
Number of Brothers and Sisters	4	26	3

If you want to change a statistics label or other attributes of a statistic (such as format, width, or decimals), select the statistic on the Cell Statistics list, edit the attributes, and click on Change. Then click on Continue to return to the main dialog box. Figure 5.3 shows the same table that you saw in Figure 5.2, with altered attributes for standard deviation.

Figure 5.3   Modified statistics attributes

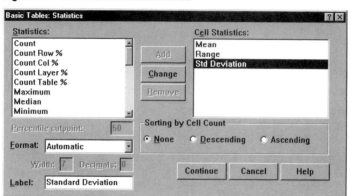

	Mean	Range	Standard Deviation
Age of Respondent	46	71	18
Highest Year of School Completed	13	20	3
Highest Year School Completed, Father	11	20	4
Highest Year School Completed, Mother	11	20	3
Highest Year School Completed, Spouse	13	20	3
Number of Children	2	8	2
Number of Brothers and Sisters	4	26	3

Subgroups with Summarized Variables

The GSS asks the respondent several questions to identify his or her occupation. From the open-ended responses to these questions, three scores are derived. The first is the U.S. Bureau of the Census three-digit occupation classification for 1980 occupations. (A simplified recoding of that variable is in the variable *occcat80*.) The second score is the two-digit Hodge, Siegel, Rossi prestige score. The third score is the U.S. Bureau of the Census three-digit industrial classification.

Do people in different occupational categories have different amounts of education? To look at occupational categories, move the variable *occcat80* to the Down list under Subgroups in the Basic Tables main dialog box. Take all of the variables except *educ* out of the Summaries list. Make sure that the current statistics are the mean, range, and standard deviation. When you click on OK, the table shown in Figure 5.4 is produced.

Figure 5.4   Summary variable with subgroups

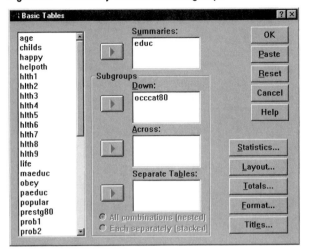

			Mean	Range	Std Deviation
Occupational Category	Managerial and Professional Specialty	Highest Year of School Completed	16	13	3
	Technical, Sales, and Administrative Support	Highest Year of School Completed	13	13	2
	Service	Highest Year of School Completed	12	15	2
	Farming, Forest, and Fishing	Highest Year of School Completed	12	17	4
	Precision Production, Craft, and Repair	Highest Year of School Completed	12	16	2
	Operation, Fabrication, and General Labor	Highest Year of School Completed	11	20	3

Here you can see that the mean education of managers and professionals is slightly higher than it is for all other job categories.

Notice that the title for the summary variable *educ* is in the column to the right of each category of the variable *occcat80*. Moving the label *Highest Year of School Completed* from the rows to the columns would make a cleaner table. Select Across the top under Summary Variable Labels in the Basic Tables Layout dialog box, and then click on Continue. This produces the table shown in Figure 5.5.

Figure 5.5   Summary variable label in columns

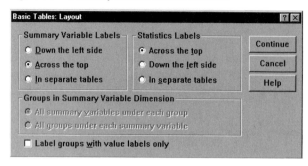

		Highest Year of School Completed		
		Mean	Range	Std Deviation
Occupational Category	Managerial and Professional Specialty	16	13	3
	Technical, Sales, and Administrative Support	13	13	2
	Service	12	15	2
	Farming, Forest, and Fishing	12	17	4
	Precision Production, Craft, and Repair	12	16	2
	Operation, Fabrication, and General Labor	11	20	3

Changing the Display Dimension of Summary Variables

Does age also vary with job category? What about prestige scores? To look at these two summary variables, replace *educ* with *age* and *prestg80*. The resulting table is shown in Figure 5.6.

Figure 5.6   Two summary variables with subgroups

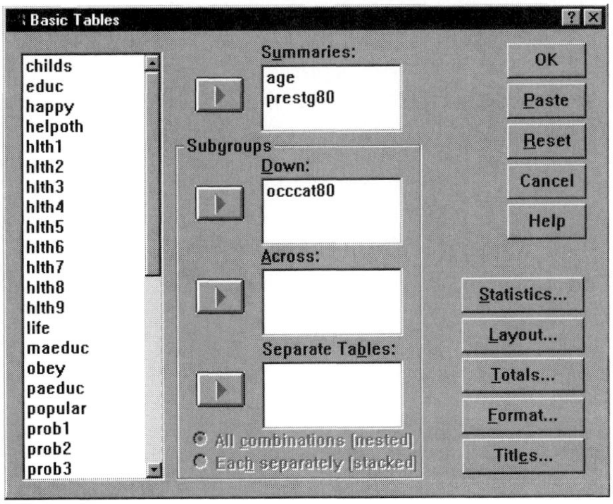

			Mean	Range	Std Deviation
Occupational Category	Managerial and Professional Specialty	Age of Respondent	45	68	16
		R's Occupational Prestige Score (1980)	59	47	9
	Technical, Sales, and Administrative Support	Age of Respondent	46	70	18
		R's Occupational Prestige Score (1980)	42	46	9
	Service	Age of Respondent	45	70	18
		R's Occupational Prestige Score (1980)	33	45	10
	Farming, Forest, and Fishing	Age of Respondent	48	63	19
		R's Occupational Prestige Score (1980)	37	27	10
	Precision Production, Craft, and Repair	Age of Respondent	47	69	18
		R's Occupational Prestige Score (1980)	42	28	7
	Operation, Fabrication, and General Labor	Age of Respondent	47	71	19
		R's Occupational Prestige Score (1980)	32	31	6

Both summary variables are nested under each category of *occcat80*. To change the position of the summary variables, click on Layout to open the Basic Tables Layout dialog box. Select All groups under each summary variable, and then click on Continue. This produces the table shown in Figure 5.7.

Figure 5.7   All groups under each summary variable

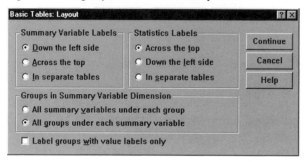

			Mean	Range	Std Deviation
Age of Respondent	Occupational Category	Managerial and Professional Specialty	45	68	16
		Technical, Sales, and Administrative Support	46	70	18
		Service	45	70	18
		Farming, Forest, and Fishing	48	63	19
		Precision Production, Craft, and Repair	47	69	18
		Operation, Fabrication, and General Labor	47	71	19
R's Occupational Prestige Score (1980)	Occupational Category	Managerial and Professional Specialty	59	47	9
		Technical, Sales, and Administrative Support	42	46	9
		Service	33	45	10
		Farming, Forest, and Fishing	37	27	10
		Precision Production, Craft, and Repair	42	28	7
		Operation, Fabrication, and General Labor	32	31	6

With only one category variable, this arrangement works well. However, with more category variables, the table could become too long. One way to prevent this is to move the summary variables to a different dimension. Select Across the top under Summary Variable Labels in the Basic Tables Layout dialog box, and then click on Continue. This produces the table shown in Figure 5.8.

Figure 5.8   Two summary variables across the top

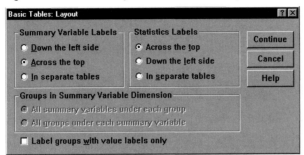

		Age of Respondent			R's Occupational Prestige Score (1980)		
		Mean	Range	Std Deviation	Mean	Range	Std Deviation
Occupational Category	Managerial and Professional Specialty	45	68	16	59	47	9
	Technical, Sales, and Administrative Support	46	70	18	42	46	9
	Service	45	70	18	33	45	10
	Farming, Forest, and Fishing	48	63	19	37	27	10
	Precision Production, Craft, and Repair	47	69	18	42	28	7
	Operation, Fabrication, and General Labor	47	71	19	32	31	6

Here you can see that the age distribution in all occupation categories is basically the same. Prestige scores are higher for managers and professionals and lower for service occupations and for operation, fabrication, and general labor occupations.

Stacking with Summarized Variables

Do people with different amounts of education differ in happiness or excitement about life? The table in Figure 5.9 shows *happy* stacked with *life* in the rows and a summary of *educ* across the top. The statistics are the mean, range, and standard deviation.

Figure 5.9   Stacking with summarized variables

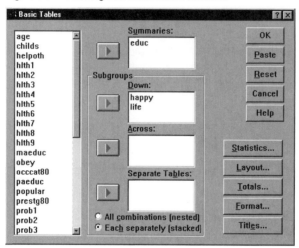

		Highest Year of School Completed		
		Mean	Range	Std Deviation
General Happiness	Very Happy	13	20	3
	Pretty Happy	13	20	3
	Not Too Happy	12	16	3
Is Life Exciting or Dull	Exciting	14	17	3
	Routine	12	20	3
	Dull	10	17	3

You can see that there is little variation in education in different categories of happiness. There is a bit more variation in the respondent's education when tabulated with excitement. The respondents who find life exciting have a mean education of 14 years, while those who find life dull have a mean education of 10 years.

Nesting with Summarized Variables

To look at interactions between education, happiness, and excitement about life, select All combinations [nested] in the Basic Tables main dialog box. This produces the table shown in Figure 5.10.

Figure 5.10 Nesting with summarized variables

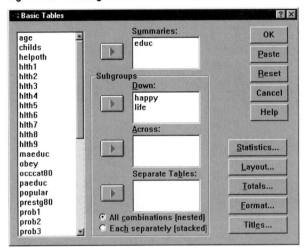

				Highest Year of School Completed		
				Mean	Range	Std Deviation
General Happiness	Very Happy	Is Life Exciting or Dull	Exciting	14	17	3
			Routine	12	16	3
			Dull	4	7	5
	Pretty Happy	Is Life Exciting or Dull	Exciting	13	16	3
			Routine	13	20	3
			Dull	11	9	3
	Not Too Happy	Is Life Exciting or Dull	Exciting	13	12	3
			Routine	12	15	3
			Dull	11	12	3

Respondents who are very happy show the strongest relationship between education and excitement about life. The education of those who are pretty happy and not too happy varies only a little between excitement categories.

Summary Variables with Totals

Now let's look at a table that shows excitement about life nested under job category. The table in Figure 5.11 shows *life* nested under *occcat80* in the rows. The summary variable, *educ*, is also in the rows. To ensure that the table is not excessively long, Down the left side is selected for summary variable labels, and All groups under each summary variable and Label groups with value labels only are selected in the Basic Tables Layout dialog box.

Figure 5.11   Excitement about life nested under occupation category

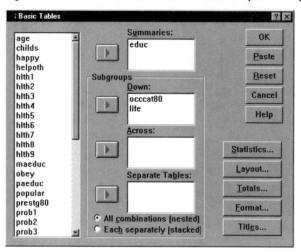

			Mean	Range	Std Deviation
Highest Year of School Completed	Managerial and Professional Specialty	Exciting	16	9	2
		Routine	15	10	2
		Dull	15	5	3
	Technical, Sales, and Administrative Support	Exciting	14	12	2
		Routine	13	11	2
		Dull	12	8	2
	Service	Exciting	12	15	3
		Routine	12	12	2
		Dull	10	5	2
	Farming, Forest, and Fishing	Exciting	12	14	4
		Routine	11	11	4
	Precision Production, Craft, and Repair	Exciting	12	11	2
		Routine	12	15	2
		Dull	10	5	2
	Operation, Fabrication, and General Labor	Exciting	11	12	3
		Routine	11	17	3
		Dull	7	12	4

Here we see the same pattern that we saw with excitement about life and job category separately. People who find life exciting have a little more education than people who find life routine, regardless of job category. People who find life routine have a little more education than people who find life dull, regardless of job category. In addition, respondents in the managerial and professional category have more education than respondents in other categories, regardless of how exciting they find life.

It might be interesting to see totals in the table in Figure 5.11. Custom Tables have a restriction on the kinds of totals that can be displayed along with nesting of variables. Because our table has *life* nested under *occcat80,* we must choose between group totals and table totals. Figure 5.12 shows group totals.

Figure 5.12   Totals of excitement nested within occupation category

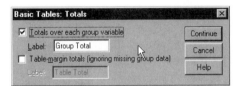

			Mean	Range	Std Deviation
Highest Year of School Completed	Managerial and Professional Specialty	Exciting	16	9	2
		Routine	15	10	2
		Dull	15	5	3
		Group Total	**16**	**10**	**2**
	Technical, Sales, and Administrative Support	Exciting	14	12	2
		Routine	13	11	2
		Dull	12	8	2
		Group Total	**13**	**13**	**2**
	Service	Exciting	12	15	3
		Routine	12	12	2
		Dull	10	5	2
		Group Total	**12**	**15**	**3**
	Farming, Forest, and Fishing	Exciting	12	14	4
		Routine	11	11	4
		Group Total	**12**	**17**	**4**
	Precision Production, Craft, and Repair	Exciting	12	11	2
		Routine	12	15	2
		Dull	10	5	2
		Group Total	**12**	**15**	**2**
	Operation, Fabrication, and General Labor	Exciting	11	12	3
		Routine	11	17	3
		Dull	7	12	4
		Group Total	**11**	**17**	**3**

Creating Categories from a Summary Variable

Sometimes the mean of a summary variable such as age doesn't quite tell you what you want. For example, the opinions of teenagers or seniors are often quite different from those of adults or children. To create a category variable from a summary variable, from the main menu select:

Transform
  Recode ▶
    Into Different Variables...

This opens the Recode into Different Variables dialog box. Select an input variable (in this case, *age*) and give the output variable a name (*agecat* would be good) and a variable label (*Age Category* would be appropriate). Click on Old and New Values to open the Recode into Different Variables Old and New Values dialog box. Select Range and enter 1 in the first text box and 12 in the second, so that it reads Range 1 through 12. Under New Value, enter 1. Now click on Add. For the second age range, enter 13 through 20. Give that a value of 2. The third age range should be 21 through 64, and the fourth should be 65 through the highest. The settings for recoding should look the same as those shown in Figure 5.13.

Figure 5.13   Recode from age to agecat

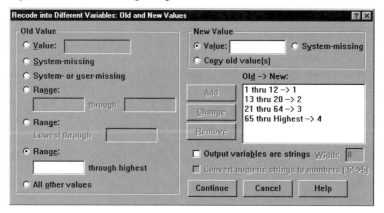

Once you have generated the new variable, use the Data Editor to give it value labels. The first category should be labeled *Child*, the second, *Teen*, the third, *Adult*, and the fourth, *Senior*. The table in Figure 5.14 shows the age category crosstabulated with the variable *happy*.

Figure 5.14   Age category crosstabulated with variable happy

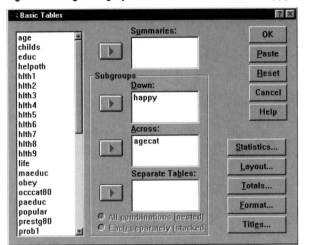

		Age Category						Table Total	
		Teen		Adult		Senior			
		Count	Col %	Count	Col %	Count	Col %	**Count**	**Col %**
General Happiness	Very Happy	6	20.7%	360	30.5%	101	34.1%	**467**	**31.1%**
	Pretty Happy	20	69.0%	694	58.9%	158	53.4%	**872**	**58.0%**
	Not Too Happy	3	10.3%	125	10.6%	37	12.5%	**165**	**11.0%**
Table Total		**30**	**100.0%**	**1189**	**100.0%**	**298**	**100.0%**	**1517**	**100.0%**

From the table, you can see that as the age category increases, so does the percentage of very happy respondents. Also, notice that no children (under 13) were surveyed, so no room is made in the table for the *Child* category.

6 Table Format Options

There are nearly as many conventions for presenting tabular data as there are people who construct tables. The format of a table may be based on aesthetic considerations, or it may be imposed by the complexity of the data. Whatever the circumstances, the Tables procedures give you a wide range of choices that can provide you with a table in nearly any format you want. This chapter describes and illustrates the range of choices by presenting the same tables in many different formats.

Suggestions for Presentation

Regardless of a table's specific purpose, some simple rules of thumb can ensure a clean table layout that shows the patterns in the data clearly. The following suggestions can help to avoid potential problems:

- *Use round numbers*. Ideally, there should be no more than two significant digits. Rounding numbers, when it does not cause distortion, simplifies mental arithmetic and makes a table easy to read. For example, it is easier to compare 46% and 38% in a column of percentages than to compare 46.45% and 38.16%. Likewise, it is easier to compare 16 and 21 in a column labeled *thousands* than to compare 15,975 and 21,482.

- *Put numbers used for comparisons close to each other in the table*. Comparisons of adjacent rows or columns can clarify complex relationships.

- *Try to arrange statistics in columns rather than rows*. That is, put the statistics labels across the top of the table rather than down the side. Reading down columns of figures is easier than reading across a row, and regularities and exceptions are more obvious. For example, it is easier to compare counts in one column and percentages in another than to view both counts and percentages interspersed in one column.

- *Use a footnote to summarize irregular or exceptional data in your table.*

- *Use a caption for notations concerning the entire table.*

- *Use grid lines or white space to separate different types of information*. Grid lines can clearly separate a few distinct items, but too many grid lines can be distracting. With many items to be separated, white space can be more effective.

- *Choose symbols and labels that are self-explanatory and easily remembered.* For example, rather than *D*, *C*, and *Y*, use *Dept.* for Department, *Corp.* for Corporation, and the unabbreviated word *Year*.

- *Use parallel labels when possible* (for example, *Retailers*, *Manufacturers*, and *Buyers* instead of *Retailers*, *Manufacturing Concerns*, and *Buys Materials*).

- *Try to keep the main dimension being compared on a single page.* If the page breaks at an awkward place, you can either make the page larger or reduce the number of items displayed in that dimension.

Setting the Default TableLook

The appearance of a table is determined by the selected default TableLook. You can choose among a collection of preset TableLooks, or you can create custom TableLooks.

To set a default TableLook, from the Viewer menus choose:

Edit
  Options...
    Pivot Tables

This opens the SPSS Options dialog box and the Pivot Tables tab, as shown in Figure 6.1.

Figure 6.1   SPSS Options Pivot Tables tab

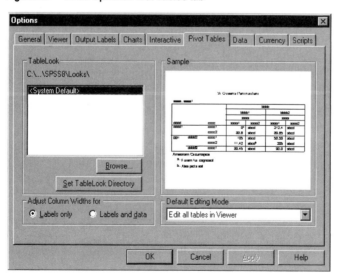

Select a TableLook from the list of files and click on OK. To select a file from another directory, click on Browse.

The next table you create will automatically be formatted with the attributes of the TableLook you selected.

Modifying a TableLook

You can modify the appearance of a single table by changing the attributes of the TableLook.

To modify a table, activate it (double-click on it) and from the Pivot Table menus choose:

Format
  Table Properties...

This opens the Table Properties dialog box, as shown in Figure 6.2. Select the attributes you want to modify and click on Apply. This gives you the opportunity to preview the table while you are modifying it. When you have achieved the look you want, click on OK. The selected attributes will be applied to the table.

Figure 6.2   Table Properties dialog box

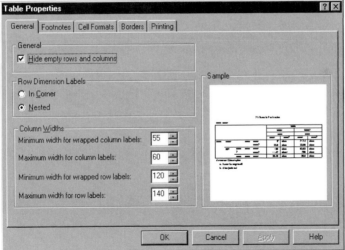

For a complete discussion of the attributes in the Table Properties dialog box, see the *SPSS Base User's Guide*. Two features deserve special note here. First, Row Dimension Labels must be set to Nested if you want to use custom corner text. Since the Custom Tables procedures do not use the corner for labeling (as many other procedures such as Crosstabs do), you might want to include this setting in a TableLook you create to apply to custom tables (see "Saving a TableLook" on p. 60). Another feature you might want to set in a TableLook is the default column widths. You can set these independently for

Column Labels (the columns containing data) and Row Labels (the leftmost columns that contain the labels for the rows). Columns that exceed the maximum you set will automatically wrap to a width no less than the minimum you set. By setting the minimum and maximum to the same value, you can make all columns the same width; a wide difference between minimum and maximum can create columns with widely varying widths.

Saving a TableLook

To create a customized TableLook, from the Pivot Table menus choose:

Format
  TableLooks...

This opens the TableLooks dialog box with <As Displayed> selected, as shown in Figure 6.3.

Figure 6.3   TableLooks dialog box

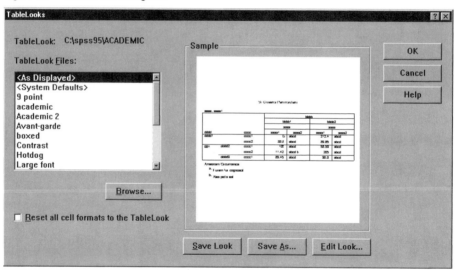

A representation of the selected TableLook appears in the sample box to the right of the selection menu.

- Click on Save Look to save the modified table properties to the currently selected TableLook file.

- Click on **Save As** to save the modified table properties to a file with a different name or directory. Use a *.tlo* extension and save it to the directory in which SPSS is installed (or the TableLook directory set in the SPSS Options Pivot Tables tab) if you want the new TableLook to appear on the TableLook Files list.
- Click on **OK** to close the dialog box.

You can reset all cells to the cell format defined by the current TableLook by selecting **Reset all cell formats to the TableLook**. This resets any cells that have been edited.

Examples of Output

The Tables procedures provide a wide range of options for presenting tabular data. There are many ways you can format a table. Using the same tables, the following examples demonstrate how to build more effective tables.

Adjusting Column Width

Each cell within a table is framed by a border. For each border location in a table, you can select a line style and a color. If you choose **None** as the style, there will be no line at the selected location. You can adjust the width of a column by clicking and dragging the border to the desired width in the Pivot Table Editor.

To set the width of data cells, from the Pivot Table menus choose:

Format
  Set Data Cell Widths...

This opens the Set Data Cell Width dialog box, as shown in Figure 6.4. The type of metrics displayed depends on the Measurement System setting in the SPSS Options General tab.

Enter the desired number of points, inches, or centimeters, or scroll to the desired number.

Figure 6.4   Set Data Cell Width dialog box

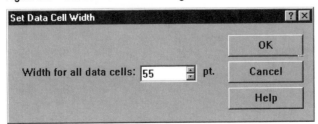

For example, the table shown in Figure 6.5 was created using the default TableLook.

Figure 6.5   Default TableLook

		Race of Respondent		
		White	Black	Other
Respondent's Sex	Male	545	71	20
	Female	719	133	29

Figure 6.6 is the same table with the data cell widths changed from 55 points to 35 points. The column label area was widened by dragging the border between *Respondent's Sex* and *Male/Female* from 72 points to 100 points.

Figure 6.6   Table with adjusted column widths

		Race of Respondent		
		White	Black	Other
Respondent's Sex	Male	545	71	20
	Female	719	133	29

For a complete discussion of setting the table properties, see the *SPSS Base User's Guide*.

Hiding Rows and Columns in a Table

You can selectively show and hide individual rows or columns in a table. To hide rows or columns in a table, [Ctrl]-[Alt]-click on the label cell of the row or column to be hidden or select that cell and from the menus choose:

Edit
  Select ▶
    Data and Label Cells

This selects the category name and the associated data cells. Once selected, they can be hidden.

For example, the table shown in Figure 6.7 was created by using the default TableLook for *occupation* by *region*.

Figure 6.7   Occupation by region

		Region of the United States		
		North East	South East	West
Occupational Category	Managerial and Professional Specialty	150	83	106
	Technical, Sales, and Administrative Support	227	109	120
	Service	87	59	58
	Farming, Forest, and Fishing	10	13	13
	Precision Production, Craft, and Repair	67	43	53
	Operation, Fabrication, and General Labor	99	77	44

If you want to hide the West region of Figure 6.7, Ctrl-Alt-click on *West*. Right-click the mouse to display the context menu. From the context menu choose **Hide Category**, or from the Pivot Table menus choose:

View
  Hide

Figure 6.8 is the same table with the West region hidden. Note that when the West region column was eliminated, the column label area was no longer large enough for the original label, *Region of the United Sates*. In this case, *United States* was changed to *U.S.* in the Pivot Table Editor. Instead of changing the title, you can make the two remaining columns wider or change the title to a smaller font.

Figure 6.8   Hidden column

		Region of the U.S.	
		North East	South East
Occupational Category	Managerial and Professional Specialty	150	83
	Technical, Sales, and Administrative Support	227	109
	Service	87	59
	Farming, Forest, and Fishing	10	13
	Precision Production, Craft, and Repair	67	43
	Operation, Fabrication, and General Labor	99	77

To show hidden rows or columns in a table, select another label in the same dimension as the hidden rows or columns. From the Pivot Table menus choose:

View
   Show All Categories in *dimension name*

The hidden row or column will again be visible. You can select:

View
   Show All

This will make all hidden rows and columns visible. If Hide empty rows and columns is selected in the Table Properties dialog box for the default TableLook, it will not show hidden empty rows or columns.

Labeling Nested Observation Variables

Figure 6.9 contains unnecessary and redundant labels.

Figure 6.9   Observation variable nested in rows with label in rows

| | | | Respondent's Sex | | | | | |
| | | | Male | | | Female | | |
			Average	Minimum	Maximum	Average	Minimum	Maximum
Occupational Category	Managerial and Professional Specialty	Age of Respondent	45	21	89	44	21	89
	Technical, Sales, and Administrative Support	Age of Respondent	42	20	83	47	19	89
	Service	Age of Respondent	43	19	81	46	19	89
	Farming, Forest, and Fishing	Age of Respondent	44	21	84	57	28	82
	Precision Production, Craft, and Repair	Age of Respondent	47	20	89	47	22	83
	Operation, Fabrication, and General Labor	Age of Respondent	43	18	82	52	20	89

Using the Basic Tables Layout dialog box, you can improve the table in several ways:

- To remove the unnecessary labels *Occupational Category* and *Respondent's Sex*, select Label groups with value labels only.

- To eliminate the repetition of *Age of Respondent*, you can either select All groups under each summary variable, which moves the label to the furthest left column, or you can select Across the top under Statistics Labels.

Figure 6.10 shows the results of these selections.

Figure 6.10   Observation variable nested in rows with label in columns

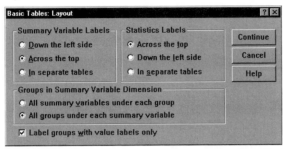

	Age of Respondent					
	Male			Female		
	Average	Minimum	Maximum	Average	Minimum	Maximum
Managerial and Professional Specialty	45	21	89	44	21	89
Technical, Sales, and Administrative Support	42	20	83	47	19	89
Service	43	19	81	46	19	89
Farming, Forest, and Fishing	44	21	84	57	28	82
Precision Production, Craft, and Repair	47	20	89	47	22	83
Operation, Fabrication, and General Labor	43	18	82	52	20	89

Labeling Nested Category Variables

Figure 6.11 shows category variables nested in rows with observation variables in columns. The category label, *Respondent's Sex*, is repeated with every pair. Review of the variations between categories is very difficult with this format.

Figure 6.11   Category variables nested in rows with observation variable in columns

				Age of Respondent	Highest Year of School Completed
Occupational Category	Managerial and Professional Specialty	Respondent's Sex	Male	45	16
			Female	44	15
	Technical, Sales, and Administrative Support	Respondent's Sex	Male	42	14
			Female	47	13
	Service	Respondent's Sex	Male	43	12
			Female	46	12
	Farming, Forest, and Fishing	Respondent's Sex	Male	44	12
			Female	57	11
	Precision Production, Craft, and Repair	Respondent's Sex	Male	47	12
			Female	47	12
	Operation, Fabrication, and General Labor	Respondent's Sex	Male	43	11
			Female	52	10

Figure 6.12 shows the same table with *Respondent's Sex* moved to the columns. You can create this table by making the same selections shown in the Basic Tables Layout dialog box (see Figure 6.10).

Figure 6.12   Category summary variable in columns

	Male		Female	
	Highest Year of School Completed	Age of Respondent	Highest Year of School Completed	Age of Respondent
Managerial and Professional Specialty	16	45	15	44
Technical, Sales, and Administrative Support	14	42	13	47
Service	12	43	12	46
Farming, Forest, and Fishing	12	44	11	57
Precision Production, Craft, and Repair	12	47	12	47
Operation, Fabrication, and General Labor	11	43	10	52

Pivoting Tables

The Pivot Table Editor enables you to rearrange your output to create desirable tables. To make the most of pivots, you will sometimes find it best to use all available table dimensions. For example, Figure 6.13 has rows defined by *sex* nested under *region*, and columns defined by *life*. The two statistics, count and row percentage, are In separate tables (or In the layer if you are using General Tables or Tables of Frequencies). You can specify the dimension for the statistics labels in the Basic Tables Layout dialog box, where you can also select Label groups with value labels only, as shown here. You can see in the pivoting window a pivot icon in each of the column, row, and layer dimensions. You can now move the statistics into any dimension you choose, and you can nest the variables under the statistics or the statistics under the variables.

Figure 6.13   Statistics in separate tables

Count

		Exciting	Routine	Dull
North East	Male	92	88	7
	Female	94	140	12
South East	Male	56	58	3
	Female	51	90	9
West	Male	65	54	2
	Female	76	75	8

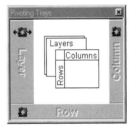

Row %

		Exciting	Routine	Dull
North East	Male	49.2%	47.1%	3.7%
	Female	38.2%	56.9%	4.9%
South East	Male	47.9%	49.6%	2.6%
	Female	34.0%	60.0%	6.0%
West	Male	53.7%	44.6%	1.7%
	Female	47.8%	47.2%	5.0%

Empty Cells and Missing Statistics

By default, empty cells are blank and missing statistics are displayed as a period. You can optionally display empty cells as 0 and represent missing statistics with any character you want. Figure 6.14 shows a default table (with empty cells displayed as blanks).

Figure 6.14   Default table

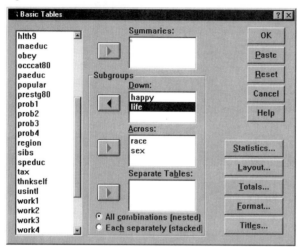

		White		Black		Other	
		Male	Female	Male	Female	Male	Female
Very Happy	Exciting	84	88	8	10	3	2
	Routine	33	51	3	8	1	2
	Dull		1	1			
Pretty Happy	Exciting	92	96	10	14	3	3
	Routine	125	154	14	31	5	9
	Dull	4	8				
Not Too Happy	Exciting	5	6	7	2	1	
	Routine	14	30	2	10	1	4
	Dull	6	14		5		1

Figure 6.15 shows the same table with 0's for empty cells and the updated Format dialog box. The Format dialog box is the same for the Basic Tables, Tables of Frequencies, and General Tables procedures.

Figure 6.15   Zeros for empty cells

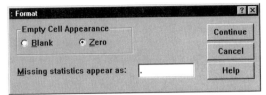

		White		Black		Other	
		Male	Female	Male	Female	Male	Female
Very Happy	Exciting	84	88	8	10	3	2
	Routine	33	51	3	8	1	2
	Dull	0	1	1	0	0	0
Pretty Happy	Exciting	92	96	10	14	3	3
	Routine	125	154	14	31	5	9
	Dull	4	8	0	0	0	0
Not Too Happy	Exciting	5	6	7	2	1	0
	Routine	14	30	2	10	1	4
	Dull	6	14	0	5	0	1

Figure 6.16 shows a similar table where missing statistics appear as *N/A*. Here, the summary variable *age* is added to the table. Notice that the cells with missing statistics are summaries of empty cells. Missing statistics are created when there aren't enough data to calculate the requested summary statistic. To improve the look of the table, the data cells were centered by changing the alignment in the Cell Properties Alignment tab on the Format menu in the Pivot Table Editor.

Figure 6.16   Missing statistics displayed as N/A

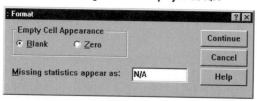

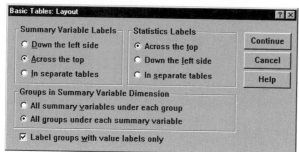

		Age of Respondent					
		White		Black		Other	
		Male	Female	Male	Female	Male	Female
Very Happy	Exciting	45	49	52	40	38	42
	Routine	47	52	53	41	31	45
	Dull	N/A	89	55	N/A	N/A	N/A
Pretty Happy	Exciting	41	43	47	44	34	43
	Routine	43	50	41	42	46	41
	Dull	53	52	N/A	N/A	N/A	N/A
Not Too Happy	Exciting	55	47	35	33	34	N/A
	Routine	41	44	30	40	49	32
	Dull	60	56	N/A	46	N/A	77

Titles and Captions

Explanatory text can be placed above or below any pivot table, regardless of the procedure used to generate it. Text above the table is called the **title**. Text below the table is called the **caption** and serves as a footnote for the entire table. Footnotes for individual data cells can be inserted in the Pivot Table Editor.

Titles

Within the Tables procedure, you can have up to 10 lines of text in a title. Each line of text is limited to 132 characters. The system will automatically wrap text to fit the width of the table. To enter a title, click on Titles to open the Titles dialog box. Enter the text in the Title text box. For example, on the first line of the Title text box, enter 1991 GSS Results. On the second line, enter Permanent survey questions. On the third line, enter Sex by Race. Figure 6.17 shows the crosstabulation of *sex* and *race* with the example title.

Figure 6.17   Table title

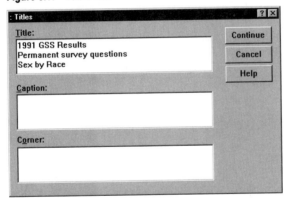

1991 GSS Results
Permanent survey questions
Sex by Race

		Race of Respondent		
		White	Black	Other
Respondent's Sex	Male	545	71	20
	Female	719	133	29

Justification (left, right, center) of the title is selected in the Table Properties Cell Formats tab on the Format menu in the Pivot Table Editor. It can be preset in the default TableLook.

Date

The function)DATE can be used in a title or a caption to print the current date. For example, Figure 6.18 shows the date added to the title. Notice that the function must be specified in upper case.

Figure 6.18   Date function in title

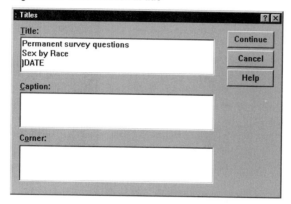

1991 GSS Results
Permanent Survey Questions
Sex by Race
09 Nov 97

	White	Black	Other	Group Total
	Count	Count	Count	Count
Male	545	71	20	636
Female	719	133	29	881
Group Total	1264	204	49	1517

The current date can be added to a caption by entering)DATE in the Caption text box. The default date format is military style; however, it can be edited in the Pivot Table Editor.

Caption

Comments that relate to the entire table can be entered in the Caption text box. You can enter up to 10 lines of text. Each line cannot exceed 132 characters. If you specify more than 10 lines of text or if any line exceeds 132 characters, the procedure issues an error message instead of producing a table. To enter a caption, click on Titles to open the Titles dialog box and enter text in the Caption text box. Figure 6.19 shows a table with the caption displayed.

Figure 6.19 Table caption

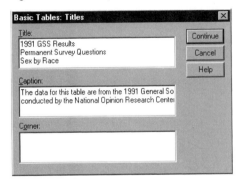

1991 GSS Results
Permanent Survey Questions
Sex by Race
09 Nov 97

	White	Black	Other	Group Total
	Count	Count	Count	Count
Male	545	71	20	636
Female	719	133	29	881
Group Total	1264	204	49	1517

The data for this table are from the 1991 General Social Survey conducted by the National Opinion Research Center.

Justification (left, right, center) of the caption is selected in the Table Properties Cell Formats tab on the Format menu in the Pivot Table Editor. It can be preset in the default TableLook.

Corners

To display comments in the area above the row labels and to the left of the column labels, enter text in the Corner text box in the Titles dialog box. You can enter up to 10 lines of text. Each line cannot exceed 65 characters. If the corner is too narrow for the text, you can widen the area by clicking and dragging the vertical category border to the desired width in the Pivot Table Editor. The height of the area is determined by the number of levels of column labels in the table.

If the portion of the table in which column titles are printed occupies too few lines, the corner lines that cannot fit will not be printed. Also, if the default TableLook uses the corner format, which reserves the corner for row dimension labels, corner text specified in the Titles dialog box will not appear. To view text in the corner, set the Row Dimension Labels as Nested in the Table Properties dialog. This option can be preset in the default TableLook.

Justification (left, right, center) of the corner text is selected in the Cell Properties Alignment tab on the Format menu in the Pivot Table Editor. It can be preset in the default TableLook.

7 Tables of Frequencies

Often a series of multiple-choice questions on a survey will all have the same choice of answers. For example, the respondent is given a list of statements and asked if he or she agrees, disagrees, or is neutral. These kinds of data are best displayed with the Tables of Frequencies procedure rather than the other two Tables procedures. In a table of frequencies, variable names appear in one dimension and the value labels for those variables appear in a different dimension. This makes it easy to display multiple variables that all share the same categories.

Building a Simple Table of Frequencies

On the GSS, there are five related questions about basic beliefs. The respondent is asked, "If you had to choose, which thing on this list would you pick as the most important for a child to learn to prepare him or her for life?" The list has five basic values: *To Obey*, *To Be Well Liked or Popular*, *To Think for One's Self*, *To Work Hard*, and *To Help Others*. The respondent is then asked which comes next in importance, which comes third, and which comes fourth. Each basic value is recorded as a different variable with values that indicate the ranking given by the respondent. The simplest table of frequencies contains a single variable for which you request frequencies. Figure 7.1 shows a table of frequencies for *obey*.

Figure 7.1   One-variable table of frequencies

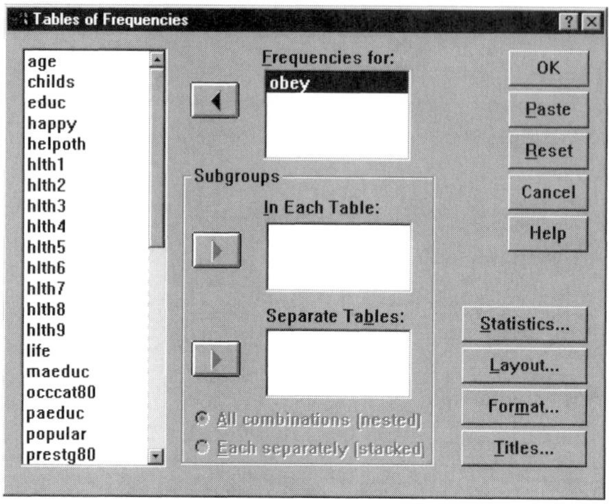

	To Obey
	Count
Most Important	195
2nd Important	123
3rd Important	142
4th Important	343
Least Important	179

Notice that this is very similar to the simplest table generated from the Basic Tables procedure, except that the variable label for *obey* is above the column of counts rather than above the value labels for *obey*. From this table, you can see that the largest number of people think obedience is fourth in importance, but a large number of people also think obedience is the most important.

We can look at the other variables by adding them to the table of frequencies. With all five variables, the table looks like the one in Figure 7.2.

Figure 7.2   Multivariable table of frequencies

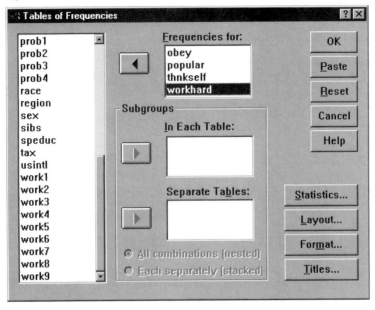

	To Obey	To Be Well Liked or Popular	To Think for Oneself	To Work Hard	To Help Others
	Count	Count	Count	Count	Count
Most Important	195	4	510	147	126
2nd Important	123	27	161	355	316
3rd Important	142	57	130	321	332
4th Important	343	185	135	144	175
Least Important	179	709	46	15	33

Again, the variable labels are above the columns and the value labels are along the side. From this table, it is clear that most people think independent thought is most important and popularity is least important. Obedience is either unimportant or most important to most people.

Adding Percentages and Totals

As with tables generated by the Basic Tables procedure, percentages sometimes add clarity to a table of frequencies. There are three statistics that can be requested in a table of frequencies: counts, percentages, and (if there is a weight variable in effect) unweighted counts. To get percentages, click on Statistics to open the Tables of Frequencies Statistics dialog box. Select Display under Percents, and change decimals for percentages from 1 to 0 in the Tables of Frequencies Statistics dialog box. Figure 7.3 shows a table with counts, percentages, and totals for all five opinion variables.

Figure 7.3   Table of frequencies with percentages

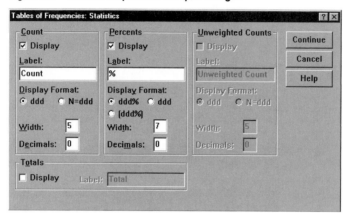

	To Obey		To Be Well Liked or Popular		To Think for Oneself		To Work Hard		To Help Others	
	Count	%	Count	%	Count	%	Count	%	Count	%
Most Important	195	20%	4	0%	510	52%	147	15%	126	13%
2nd Important	123	13%	27	3%	161	16%	355	36%	316	32%
3rd Important	142	14%	57	6%	130	13%	321	33%	332	34%
4th Important	343	35%	185	19%	135	14%	144	15%	175	18%
Least Important	179	18%	709	72%	46	5%	15	2%	33	3%
Total	982	100%	982	100%	982	100%	982	100%	982	100%

You can see that 52% of the respondents believe that *To Think for One's Self* is most important. Seventy-two percent believe that *To Be Well Liked or Popular* is least important. Since the frequency variables form columns, column percentages are shown. The percentages for each frequency variable thus add up to 100%.

Notice that the percentage rows also add up to 100%. This is because of the data, not the percentage type. The data are a ranking of five opinions. If one respondent chooses *To Think for One's Self* as most important, that same respondent cannot also choose *To Obey* as most important. The total number of respondents who rank something as most important is equal to the total number of respondents in the survey. If the table shows only a few of the opinion variables, the percentage rows will no longer add up to 100%.

Adding Subgroups

Does this pattern of beliefs vary with other characteristics of the respondents, such as sex, race, and region? To look at interactions between the frequency variables and these characteristics, you need to divide the frequency variables into subgroups. The table in Figure 7.4 shows the frequency variables *obey*, *popular*, and *thnkself* broken into subgroups by *sex*.

Figure 7.4   Table of frequencies with subgroups

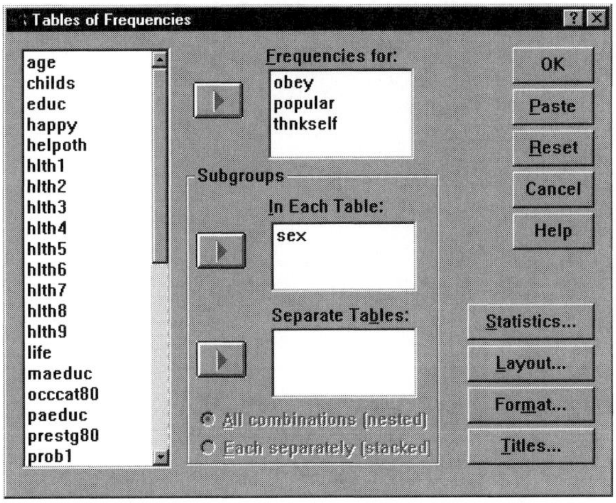

	Respondent's Sex											
	Male						Female					
	To Obey		To Be Well Liked or Popular		To Think for Oneself		To Obey		To Be Well Liked or Popular		To Think for Oneself	
	Count	%	Count	%	Count	%	Count	%	Count	%	Count	%
Most Important	87	21%	2	0%	193	47%	108	19%	2	0%	317	55%
2nd Important	53	13%	15	4%	79	19%	70	12%	12	2%	82	14%
3rd Important	62	15%	33	8%	52	13%	80	14%	24	4%	78	14%
4th Important	123	30%	83	20%	61	15%	220	38%	102	18%	74	13%
Least Important	83	20%	275	67%	23	6%	96	17%	434	76%	23	4%
Total	**408**	**100%**	**408**	**100%**	**408**	**100%**	**574**	**100%**	**574**	**100%**	**574**	**100%**

In this table, you can see the same pattern for both males and females. *To Think for One's Self* is most important for most people; *To Be Well Liked or Popular* is least important; and *To Obey* is a low priority for most, but to a sizable number, it is most important.

Altering the Layout

In all the frequency tables so far, frequency variable labels appear across the top of the table and their value labels appear down the side. This emphasizes the ranking rather than the categories. To emphasize the categories, move the frequency variables to the rows. This is done with the Tables of Frequencies Layout dialog box. The table in Figure 7.5 is the same as that shown in Figure 7.4, except that frequency variables are now in rows down the side.

Figure 7.5   Table of frequencies with variable labels down the side

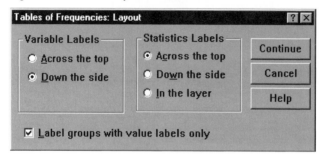

		Most Important		2nd Important		3rd Important		4th Important		Least Important	
		Count	%	Count	%	Count	%	Count	%	Count	%
Male	To Obey	87	21%	53	13%	62	15%	123	30%	83	20%
	To Be Well Liked or Popular	2	0%	15	4%	33	8%	83	20%	275	67%
	To Think for Oneself	193	47%	79	19%	52	13%	61	15%	23	6%
Female	To Obey	108	19%	70	12%	80	14%	220	38%	96	17%
	To Be Well Liked or Popular	2	0%	12	2%	24	4%	102	18%	434	76%
	To Think for Oneself	317	55%	82	14%	78	14%	74	13%	23	4%

Variable labels are now down the side and value labels are across the top. Notice that the percentages still add up to 100% for each frequency variable. When the position of the frequency variables changes from columns to rows, the percentages change from column percentages to row percentages.

Stacking Subgroups

The previous tables show *opinion* by *sex*. Both male and female respondents find independent thought most important and popularity least important. Both sexes are split on obedience. How about *opinion* by *race* and *region*? Is the pattern the same? Figure 7.6 shows *race* and *region* stacked in the columns with frequencies for *obey, popular,* and *thnkself.*

Figure 7.6   Table of frequencies with stacked subgroups

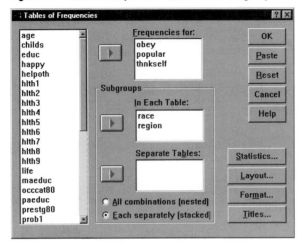

		White			Black			Other			North East			South East			West		
		To Obey	To Be Well Liked or Popular	To Think for Oneself	To Obey	To Be Well Liked or Popular	To Think for Oneself	To Obey	To Be Well Liked or Popular	To Think for Oneself	To Obey	To Be Well Liked or Popular	To Think for Oneself	To Obey	To Be Well Liked or Popular	To Think for Oneself	To Obey	To Be Well Liked or Popular	To Think for Oneself
Most Important	Count	148	4	450	38		52	9		8	77	1	245	68	1	123	50	2	142
	%	18%	0%	55%	28%		39%	30%		27%	17%	0%	54%	26%	0%	47%	19%	1%	53%
2nd Important	Count	89	15	131	31	9	24	3	3	6	55	12	74	40	9	42	28	6	45
	%	11%	2%	16%	23%	7%	18%	10%	10%	20%	12%	3%	16%	15%	3%	16%	10%	2%	17%
3rd Important	Count	124	44	101	11	10	23	7	3	6	65	25	64	39	10	38	38	22	28
	%	15%	5%	12%	8%	7%	17%	23%	10%	20%	14%	6%	14%	15%	4%	14%	14%	8%	10%
4th Important	Count	297	163	101	39	17	27	7	5	7	169	87	51	77	47	47	97	51	37
	%	36%	20%	12%	29%	13%	20%	23%	17%	23%	37%	19%	11%	29%	18%	18%	36%	19%	14%
Least Important	Count	159	591	34	16	99	9	4	19	3	85	326	17	39	196	13	55	187	16
	%	19%	72%	4%	12%	73%	7%	13%	63%	10%	19%	72%	4%	15%	75%	5%	21%	70%	6%

Column group headers: "Race of Respondent" spans White, Black, Other. "Region of the United States" spans North East, South East, West.

From this table, we can see similar patterns in all categories, although larger percentages of blacks and people in the Southeast find obedience most important than respondents in other categories. (The number of respondents in the *Other* category is so small that it is hard to draw generalizations from those results.)

Notice that this table is very wide. To produce tables that are easier to read with the same information, you could print two separate tables (with one broken down by *race* and the other broken down by *region*) or place the variable labels down the side.

Nesting Subgroups

In the last table, we noticed that nonwhites and people in the Southeast show a similar pattern of *opinion* that is slightly different from that of whites or people in other regions. Is this because the same respondents are in both groups, or do separate respondents in the two groups show the same pattern? Figure 7.7 shows *region* nested under *race*. The only frequency variable shown is *obey*.

Figure 7.7   Table of frequencies with nested subgroups

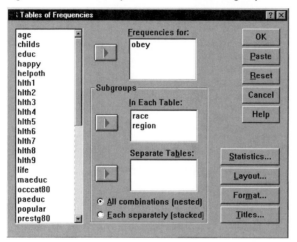

		Race of Respondent								
		White			Black			Other		
		Region of the United States			Region of the United States			Region of the United States		
		North East	South East	West	North East	South East	West	North East	South East	West
		To Obey	To Obey	To Obey	To Obey	To Obey	To Obey	To Obey	To Obey	To Obey
Most Important	Count	61	46	41	12	19	7	4	3	2
	%	16%	23%	18%	22%	32%	32%	44%	43%	14%
2nd Important	Count	45	24	20	10	14	7		2	1
	%	12%	12%	9%	19%	24%	32%		29%	7%
3rd Important	Count	61	30	33	3	8		1	1	5
	%	16%	15%	14%	6%	14%		11%	14%	36%
4th Important	Count	147	63	87	20	13	6	2	1	4
	%	38%	32%	38%	37%	22%	27%	22%	14%	29%
Least Important	Count	74	34	51	9	5	2	2		2
	%	19%	17%	22%	17%	8%	9%	22%		14%

Here you can see that a larger proportion of whites and blacks in the Southeast finds obedience most important. Also, a larger proportion of blacks than whites in all regions finds obedience most important. It appears that respondents in the two groups share similar opinions.

Notice that the column titles in Figure 7.7 would look less cluttered and still be just as informative if groups were labeled with only value labels.

Subgroups in the Layers Dimension

If you want to add the *sex* variable to the analysis, you can put *sex* on the Separate Tables list under Subgroups. The table is shown in two layers in Figure 7.8. Each sex is a separate layer. *Region* is nested under *race* in the columns. The frequency variable labels are in the columns, while the value labels and statistics labels are in the rows. All subgroups are labeled with value labels only. Notice that since the percentages are column percentages, each column adds up to 100% across the layers.

The number of respondents in each cell in Figure 7.8 is fairly small (there are 90 cells in the table), so the applicability of the results to the U.S. population as a whole is suspect. Even so, it appears that the pattern observed for *opinion* by *race* and *region* does not differ for the two sexes.

Figure 7.8   Table of frequencies with subgroups in separate layers

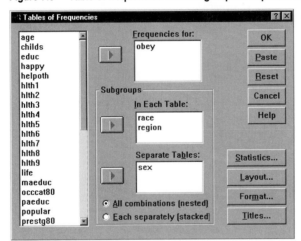

Respondent's Sex Male

		Race of Respondent								
		White			Black			Other		
		Region of the United States			Region of the United States			Region of the United States		
		North East	South East	West	North East	South East	West	North East	South East	West
		To Obey	To Obey	To Obey	To Obey	To Obey	To Obey	To Obey	To Obey	To Obey
Most Important	Count	32	22	18	3	5	3	1	2	1
	%	8%	11%	8%	6%	8%	14%	11%	29%	7%
2nd Important	Count	21	13	8	3	6	1			1
	%	5%	7%	3%	6%	10%	5%			7%
3rd Important	Count	24	14	15	2	5				2
	%	6%	7%	6%	4%	8%				14%
4th Important	Count	49	27	31	8	1	3		1	3
	%	13%	14%	13%	15%	2%	14%		14%	21%
Least Important	Count	37	15	20	4	4	1	2		
	%	10%	8%	9%	7%	7%	5%	22%		

Respondent's Sex Female

		Race of Respondent								
		White			Black			Other		
		Region of the United States			Region of the United States			Region of the United States		
		North East	South East	West	North East	South East	West	North East	South East	West
		To Obey	To Obey	To Obey	To Obey	To Obey	To Obey	To Obey	To Obey	To Obey
Most Important	Count	29	24	23	9	14	4	3	1	1
	%	7%	12%	10%	17%	24%	18%	33%	14%	7%
2nd Important	Count	24	11	12	7	8	6		2	
	%	6%	6%	5%	13%	14%	27%		29%	
3rd Important	Count	37	16	18	1	3		1	1	3
	%	10%	8%	8%	2%	5%		11%	14%	21%
4th Important	Count	98	36	56	12	12	3	2		1
	%	25%	18%	24%	22%	20%	14%	22%		7%
Least Important	Count	37	19	31	5	1	1			2
	%	10%	10%	13%	9%	2%	5%			14%

8 Multiple-Response Questions

The information sought by survey and market researchers often requires questions to which a respondent can give multiple responses. For instance, survey questions often ask respondents to indicate which magazines they read or to rank in importance a list of political issues. A single variable cannot record the answers to these types of questions adequately, since a variable can have only one value for each case.

The solution is to record the responses in multiple variables, and then count across the multiple variables and report the results as if they were a single variable. This chapter describes how to code multiple-response questions and how to analyze them with the Multiple Response Tables procedure.

Coding Multiple-Response Items

The General Social Survey (GSS) includes a series of questions that asks respondents about their problems. The survey poses the same basic question in two different ways. First, respondents are asked an open-ended question to which multiple responses may be given. Then, respondents are asked a set of specific questions to which they may respond either "yes" or "no." These two forms of survey questions illustrate the two methods by which a multiple-response question may be coded.

For example, the survey asks the open-ended question "What are the most important problems that you and members of your household have had during the last 12 months?" The respondent's answer is recorded verbatim. After the interview, the answers are coded for statistical analysis. The answer is subdivided into four variables, each with 100 possible problems listed. If the answer lists one problem, that problem is coded in the first variable. If the answer lists two problems, they are coded in the first and second variable, and so on. If more than four problems are listed, only the first four are recorded. This is called a multiple-response question **coded as categories**.

Next, the survey poses a set of specific questions on the same topic, including the following question:

First, thinking about health-related matters, did any of the following happen to you since February/March, 1990?

1. Ill enough to go to a doctor.

2. Underwent counseling for mental or emotional problems.

3. Infertility or unable to have a baby....

Each of these questions is recorded as a single variable that can have one of two values—"yes" or "no/no answer/not applicable." This set of questions is called a multiple-response question **coded as dichotomies**.

Defining Multiple-Response Sets

Before multiple-response variables can be used in a table, they must be defined as a multiple-response set. To define a multiple-response set, open the Multiple Response Tables dialog box and click on Mult Response Sets. This opens the Multiple Response Tables Define Multiple-Response Sets dialog box. From here you can define the multiple-response set.

Defining Sets as Categories

If your multiple-response variables are coded as categories, move each multicategory variable from the source variable list to the Variables in Set list. For example, the multicategory variables on the GSS are the variables *prob1* through *prob4*, as shown in Figure 8.1.

Figure 8.1   Definition for multiple-response set as categories

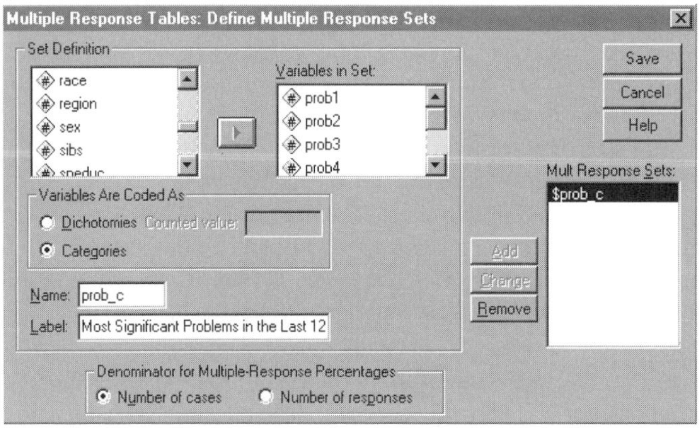

Select Categories under Variables Are Coded As, and then give the new multiple-response set a name. For example, the list of problems coded as categories could be called *prob_c*. The multiple-response set name follows normal variable-naming conventions, except that it can be only seven characters long. You can also give the multiple-response set a variable label. For example, *Most Significant Problems in the Last 12 Months* would be a good label for *prob_c*.

When you click on **Add**, the new multiple-response set name appears on the Mult Response Sets list with a dollar sign ($) preceding it. (The dollar sign indicates that it is a multiple-response set.) When you click on **Save**, the variables on the Mult Response Sets list appear on the Multiple Response Sets list in the Multiple Response Tables dialog box. You can select variables from this list and move them into rows, columns, or layers, as with normal variables. When you save your data file, the set definitions are also saved, so the sets will be available when you use Tables again with the same SPSS data file.

The variables *prob1* through *prob4* on the original GSS each have 100 categories. To make these variables more manageable, they are recoded into seven general categories in *1991 U.S. General Social Survey.sav*. These categories are health, finances, lack of basic services, family, personal, legal, and miscellaneous.

Defining Sets as Dichotomies

If your multiple-response variables are coded as dichotomies, move each dichotomy variable from the source variable list to the Variables in Set list. The GSS has about 50 dichotomous variables that record specific problems. So that the tables generated are more manageable, *1991 U.S. General Social Survey.sav* contains only the first 18 variables. This includes all of the health-related and work-related questions. Select the variables *hlth1* through *hlth9* and *work1* through *work9* and move them to the Variables in Set list, as shown in Figure 8.2.

Figure 8.2   Definition for multiple-response set as dichotomies

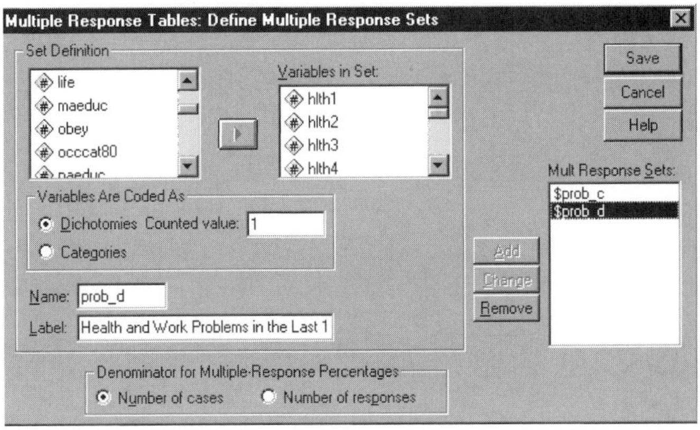

Make sure that **Dichotomies** under Variables Are Coded As is selected. Next, enter a number for the Counted value text box. This is where you tell the General Tables procedure which value you are interested in. For example, on the GSS, the respondent can answer a dichotomous question "yes," "no," or give no answer; or the question might not apply to the respondent for some reason. A "yes" is coded 1, a "no" is coded 2, "no response" is coded 9, and "not applicable" is coded 0. We want to look only at "yes" answers. For our purposes, "no," "no response," and "not applicable" are all equivalent—they are not "yes." Enter a 1 for "yes" in the Counted value text box.

Now give the new multiple-response set a name. For example, the set of problem dichotomies could be called *prob_d*. The multiple-response set name follows normal variable-naming conventions, except that it can be only seven characters long. You can also give the multiple-response set a variable label. For example, *Health and Work Problems in the Last 12 Months* is an appropriate label for *prob_d*.

When you click on Add, the new multiple-response set name appears on the Mult Response Sets list with a dollar sign preceding it. When you click on Save, the variables on the Mult Response Sets list appear on the Multiple Response Sets list in the Multiple Response Tables dialog box. You can select variables from this list and move them into rows, columns, or layers, as with normal variables. When you save your data file, the set definitions are also saved, so the sets will be available when you use Tables again with the same SPSS data file.

Using Multiple-Response Sets

Under most circumstances, a multiple-response set can be treated just like a normal categorical variable. For example, Figure 8.3 shows the multiple-response variable *$prob_c* (coded as categories) in the rows dimension crosstabulated with *happy* in the columns dimension.

Figure 8.3   Multiple-response set coded as categories

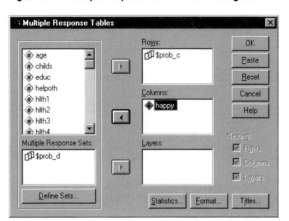

		General Happiness		
		Very Happy	Pretty Happy	Not Too Happy
Most Significant Problems in the Last 12 Months	Health	38	75	23
	Finances	37	130	36
	Lack of Basic Services	2	5	
	Family	15	44	16
	Personal	11	24	6
	Legal	1	1	
	Miscellaneous	17	43	11

Figure 8.4 shows the multiple-response variable *$prob_d* (coded as dichotomies) in the rows dimension crosstabulated with *happy* in the columns dimension.

Figure 8.4   Multiple-response set coded as dichotomies

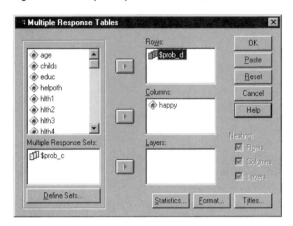

		General Happiness		
		Very Happy	Pretty Happy	Not Too Happy
Health and Work Problems in the Last 12 Months	Ill Enough to Go to a Doctor	171	316	68
	Counselling for Mental Problems	9	39	10
	Infertility, Unable to Have a Baby	9	24	2
	Drinking Problem	2	9	6
	Illegal Drugs (Marijuana, Cocaine)	4	13	13
	Partner (Husband, Wife) In Hospital	21	36	15
	Child in Hospital	23	37	16
	Child on Drugs, Drinking Problem	5	17	6
	Death of a Close Friend	77	124	27
	Unemployed and Looking for Work a Month +	9	38	11
	Being Demoted or Move to Worse Position	5	12	7
	Cut in Pay or Reduced Hours	14	34	12
	Being Passed Over for Promotion	9	24	5
	Having Trouble with One's Boss	12	24	5
	Own Business Losing Money or Failing	2	13	5
	Partner (Husband, Wife) Being Fired	8	15	2
	Partner (Husband, Wife) Cut in Pay	12	36	3
	One's Spouse Being Unemployed	14	37	4

Percentages with Multiple-Response Sets

By definition, the number of responses can be greater than the number of cases in a multiple-response set (each respondent can give more than one answer). This creates two ways of calculating percentages: they can be based on the total responses received or on the number of cases. By default, they are based on cases. For example, starting with the table as specified in Figure 8.3, click Statistics and request Counts, Column Percentages, and Totals, as shown in Figure 8.5.

Figure 8.5   Percentages based on cases

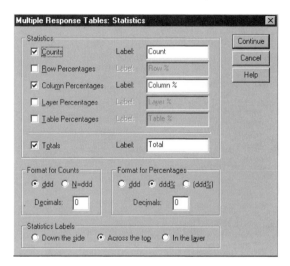

		General Happiness						Total	
		Very Happy		Pretty Happy		Not Too Happy			
		Count	Column %	Count	Column %	Count	Column %	Count	Column %
Most Significant Problems in the Last 12 Months	Health	38	47.5	75	37.1	23	47.9	136	41.2
	Finances	37	46.3	130	64.4	36	75.0	203	61.5
	Lack of Basic Services	2	2.5	5	2.5			7	2.1
	Family	15	18.8	44	21.8	16	33.3	75	22.7
	Personal	11	13.8	24	11.9	6	12.5	41	12.4
	Legal	1	1.3	1	.5			2	.6
	Miscellaneous	17	21.3	43	21.3	11	22.9	71	21.5
Total		**80**	**100.0**	**202**	**100.0**	**48**	**100.0**	**330**	**100.0**

Notice that in Figure 8.5, the column totals are considerably smaller than the sum of the column contents. The total number of responses for *Very Happy* is 121, but the total in that column is 80. That is because the count statistic for a multiple-response variable is a count of cases. Each case can contribute more than one response and can thus appear in more than one cell of the table. But each case can appear only once in the total of cases. Thus, the table shows, for example, that out of 80 respondents who described themselves as very happy, 38 (or 48%) mentioned health as a significant problem in the last 12 months. If you want to see the total number of responses and the percentage that total is of the total number of cases, you can use the General Tables procedure and choose **Responses** and **Response percentages** for your statistics.

If you want percentages based on the number of responses, return to the Define Multiple Response Sets dialog box. Under Denominator for Multiple-Response Percentages, select **Number of responses** and click **Save**. The same table is generated, except that column percentages are lower, totaling 61.7%, as shown in Figure 8.6. The 66% now showing as the *Total Column %* for the *Very Happy* group represents the number of cases in that group (80) as a percentage of the number of responses in that group (121).

Figure 8.6   Responses add up to 100%

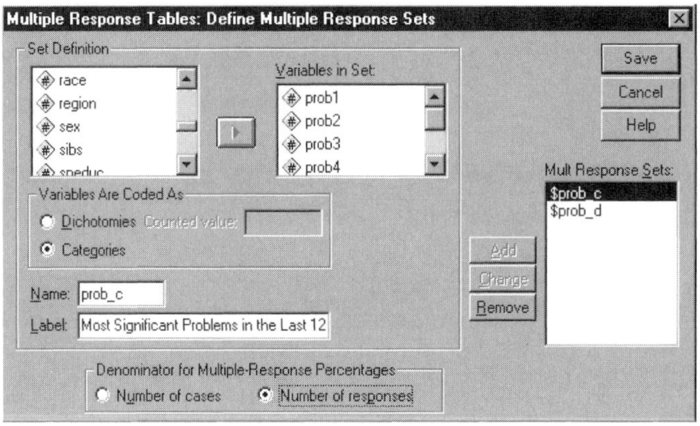

| | | General Happiness | | | | | | Total | |
| | | Very Happy | | Pretty Happy | | Not Too Happy | | | |
		Count	Column %	Count	Column %	Count	Column %	Count	Column %
Most Significant Problems in the Last 12 Months	Health	38	31.4	75	23.3	23	25.0	136	25.4
	Finances	37	30.6	130	40.4	36	39.1	203	37.9
	Lack of Basic Services	2	1.7	5	1.6			7	1.3
	Family	15	12.4	44	13.7	16	17.4	75	14.0
	Personal	11	9.1	24	7.5	6	6.5	41	7.7
	Legal	1	.8	1	.3			2	.4
	Miscellaneous	17	14.0	43	13.4	11	12.0	71	13.3
Total		**80**	**66.1**	**202**	**62.7**	**48**	**52.2**	**330**	**61.7**

The General Tables procedure also handles multiple-response sets and offers increased flexibility in choosing statistics and totals to display. Figure 8.7 shows the same table as Figure 8.5, but with Responses and Response Col % selected as statistics for *prob_c*. The individual cells show the same counts, but the totals are based on the total number of responses, which can (and usually does) exceed the number of respondents. The totals for column percentages now provide the information that, on average, very happy people named 1.5 significant problems, while not too happy people named 1.9.

Figure 8.7   Response totals from General Tables

		General Happiness					
		Very Happy		Pretty Happy		Not Too Happy	
		Responses	Col Response %	Responses	Col Response %	Responses	Col Response %
Most Significant Problems in the Last 12 Months	Health	38	47.5%	75	37.1%	23	47.9%
	Finances	37	46.3%	130	64.4%	36	75.0%
	Lack of Basic Services	2	2.5%	5	2.5%		
	Family	15	18.8%	44	21.8%	16	33.3%
	Personal	11	13.8%	24	11.9%	6	12.5%
	Legal	1	1.3%	1	.5%		
	Miscellaneous	17	21.3%	43	21.3%	11	22.9%
Total		121	151.3%	322	159.4%	92	191.7%

9 Stacking and Nesting in General Tables

For many tables, the Basic Tables and Multiple Response Tables procedures give you enough flexibility and are easier to use than the General Tables procedure. However, for tables that require both stacking and nesting of variables, different statistics for different variables, or complex totals, the General Tables procedure is required. This chapter introduces the General Tables procedure and provides examples of several tables that could also be constructed with the Basic Tables procedure. After the introduction, mixed stacking and nesting is explained. Chapter 10 describes how to use summary statistics with the General Tables procedure. Chapter 11 describes how to get totals for the General Tables procedure. For information on how to code and use multiple-response variables, see Chapter 8.

A Simple One-Dimensional Table

The simplest table has one dimension. Figure 9.1 shows a one-dimensional table with the variable *happy* in the rows.

Figure 9.1   Simple one-dimensional table

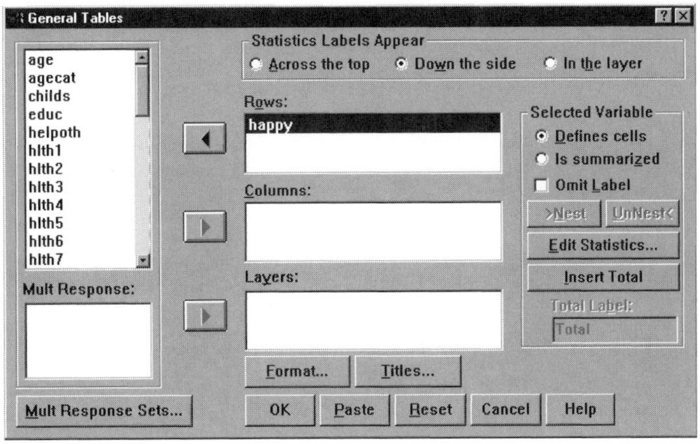

General Happiness	Very Happy	467
	Pretty Happy	872
	Not Too Happy	165

You can stack more than one variable in the same dimension by adding additional variables to the same list, as shown in Figure 9.2.

Figure 9.2   Stacked variables

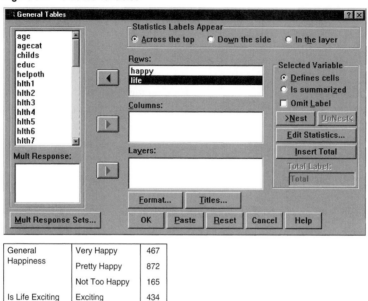

General Happiness	Very Happy	467
	Pretty Happy	872
	Not Too Happy	165
Is Life Exciting or Dull	Exciting	434
	Routine	505
	Dull	41

Adding Dimensions

You can add a second dimension by moving one or more variables to the Columns list, as shown in Figure 9.3. A two-dimensional table is called a **crosstabulation**. In the table shown in Figure 9.3, *happy* is crosstabulated with *race*, and *life* is also crosstabulated with *race*.

Figure 9.3   Two-dimensional table

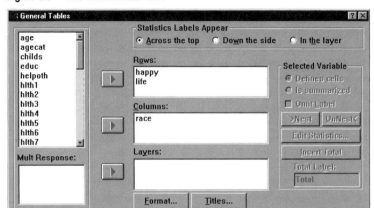

		Race of Respondent		
		White	Black	Other
General Happiness	Very Happy	409	46	12
	Pretty Happy	730	116	26
	Not Too Happy	117	39	9
Is Life Exciting or Dull	Exciting	371	51	12
	Routine	413	69	23
	Dull	34	6	1

To create a third dimension, add one or more variables to the Layers list, as shown in Figure 9.4. SPSS generates a separate table that crosstabulates row and column variables for each layer variable.

Figure 9.4   Three-dimensional table

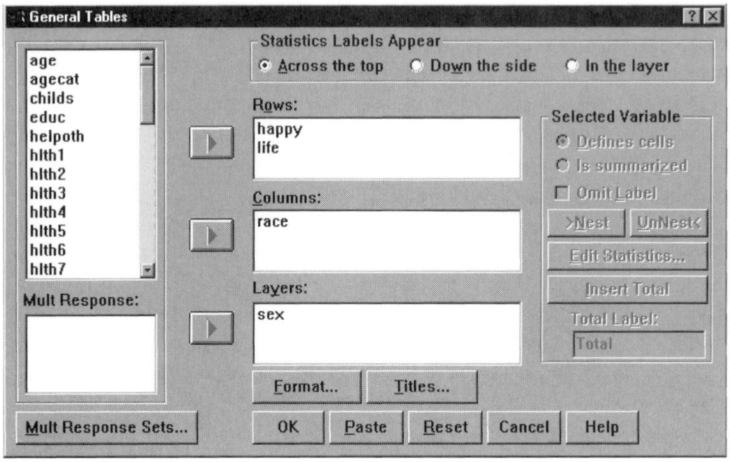

Respondent's Sex Male

		Race of Respondent		
		White	Black	Other
General Happiness	Very Happy	180	19	7
	Pretty Happy	326	38	10
	Not Too Happy	37	13	3
Is Life Exciting or Dull	Exciting	181	25	7
	Routine	173	20	7
	Dull	11	1	

Respondent's Sex Female

		Race of Respondent		
		White	Black	Other
General Happiness	Very Happy	229	27	5
	Pretty Happy	404	78	16
	Not Too Happy	80	26	6
Is Life Exciting or Dull	Exciting	190	26	5
	Routine	240	49	16
	Dull	23	5	1

Nesting and Stacking

The table in Figure 9.4 compares happiness and excitement about life with race and sex. The variables *happy* and *life* are in the rows, *race* is in the columns, and *sex* is in the layers. This table, and all the tables illustrated so far, can also be produced with the Basic Tables procedure.

However, what if you want to combine the data from the two tables in Figure 9.4 into a single table? Using the General Tables procedure, you can combine them by nesting the variables. **Nesting** is a way to compress two dimensions into a single dimension or a way to break summary variables into categories, where all categories of the nested variable are displayed for each category of the variable above it. Nesting allows you to create a single table that is easier to interpret. You can nest variables only with the General Tables procedure.

For example, suppose you want to nest *sex* under *race* in the columns, but you don't want to nest *happy* and *life*? Simply place the variables in the proper dimensions, and then select *sex* and click on Nest. Notice that *sex* is now indented on the Columns list. The table that will be generated is shown in Figure 9.5.

Figure 9.5   Mixed nesting and stacking

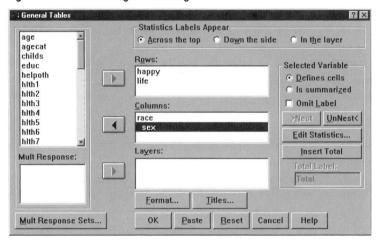

		Race of Respondent					
		White		Black		Other	
		Respondent's Sex		Respondent's Sex		Respondent's Sex	
		Male	Female	Male	Female	Male	Female
General Happiness	Very Happy	180	229	19	27	7	5
	Pretty Happy	326	404	38	78	10	16
	Not Too Happy	37	80	13	26	3	6
Is Life Exciting or Dull	Exciting	181	190	25	26	7	5
	Routine	173	240	20	49	7	16
	Dull	11	23	1	5		1

This table compares the same statistics as the table in Figure 9.4, but the arrangement makes it easier to compare responses across sexes. The reported level of happiness seems fairly consistent across *race* and *sex*. A larger number of men find life more exciting than routine or dull, and a larger number of women find life more routine than exciting or dull.

You can achieve the same effect by using the Pivot Table Editor on the table illustrated in Figure 9.4. Move the layer icon from the layer dimension to the column dimension.

Figure 9.6 shows nesting and stacking in the same dimension. *Happy* is stacked with *life*, and both are nested under *region* in the rows. *Sex* is nested under *race* in the columns.

Figure 9.6   Nesting and stacking in the same dimension

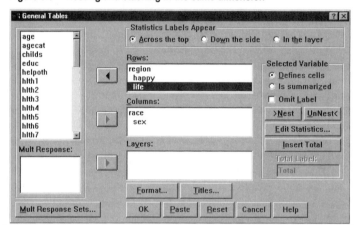

				Race of Respondent					
				White		Black		Other	
				Respondent's Sex		Respondent's Sex		Respondent's Sex	
				Male	Female	Male	Female	Male	Female
Region of the United States	North East	General Happiness	Very Happy	69	93	6	12	3	2
			Pretty Happy	160	201	14	30	2	5
			Not Too Happy	19	36	7	12		2
		Is Life Exciting or Dull	Exciting	83	79	7	12	2	3
			Routine	74	116	11	21	3	3
			Dull	6	10	1	2		
	South East	General Happiness	Very Happy	57	66	10	13	3	
			Pretty Happy	70	80	21	35	3	6
			Not Too Happy	10	21	2	12		2
		Is Life Exciting or Dull	Exciting	41	38	12	12	3	1
			Routine	49	62	8	22	1	6
			Dull	3	6		3		
	West	General Happiness	Very Happy	54	70	3	2	1	3
			Pretty Happy	96	123	3	13	5	5
			Not Too Happy	8	23	4	2	3	2
		Is Life Exciting or Dull	Exciting	57	73	6	2	2	1
			Routine	50	62	1	6	3	7
			Dull	2	7				1

Multiple Nesting Levels

You can also add more than one level of nesting within each dimension of a table. For example, in Figure 9.7, *life* is nested beneath *happy*, which is nested beneath *region*. To add multiple nesting levels, simply select each variable and click on Nest. On the list, each nested variable will appear indented beneath the variable above it. This table can also be produced using the Basic Tables procedure because each variable is nested beneath the previous variable on the same list. (The variable under which another variable is nested is called the **controlling variable**.)

Figure 9.7   Multiple levels of nesting

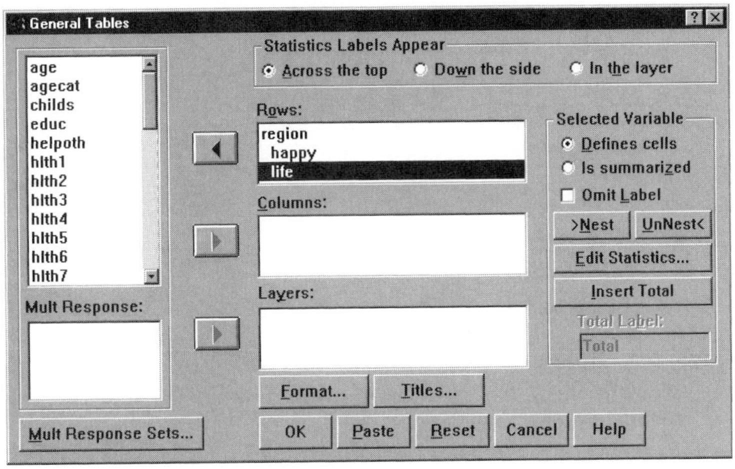

Figure 9.7   Multiple levels of nesting (Continued)

Region of the United States	North East	General Happiness	Very Happy	Is Life Exciting or Dull	Exciting	80
					Routine	40
					Dull	1
			Pretty Happy	Is Life Exciting or Dull	Exciting	99
					Routine	159
					Dull	6
			Not Too Happy	Is Life Exciting or Dull	Exciting	7
					Routine	25
					Dull	12
	South East	General Happiness	Very Happy	Is Life Exciting or Dull	Exciting	52
					Routine	33
					Dull	1
			Pretty Happy	Is Life Exciting or Dull	Exciting	51
					Routine	89
					Dull	3
			Not Too Happy	Is Life Exciting or Dull	Exciting	4
					Routine	23
					Dull	8
	West	General Happiness	Very Happy	Is Life Exciting or Dull	Exciting	63
					Routine	25
			Pretty Happy	Is Life Exciting or Dull	Exciting	68
					Routine	90
					Dull	3
			Not Too Happy	Is Life Exciting or Dull	Exciting	10
					Routine	13
					Dull	6

Adding Statistics

With the Basic Tables procedure, you select statistics for the whole table. With the General Tables procedure, you select statistics for each variable independently. Figure 9.8 shows a table with *happy* and *life* stacked in the rows and *sex* nested under *race* in the columns. This table is similar to the table in Figure 9.5, except that counts and column percentages are shown for the variable *happy*. To get statistics for a specific variable, select the variable and click on **Edit Statistics** to open the General Tables Cell Statistics dialog box. Select the statistics and click on **OK**.

When you return to the main dialog box, notice that the options under Statistics Labels Appear are disabled. This is because different variables stacked in the same dimension now have different statistics (*happy* has counts and column percentages, while *life* has counts only). If the statistics labels were allowed in the columns, the percentage column would be empty for *life*. Instead, the statistics labels automatically appear in the same dimension as the variables with the different statistics (the rows). When you click on **OK**, the program produces the table shown in Figure 9.8.

Figure 9.8 Percentages for one variable

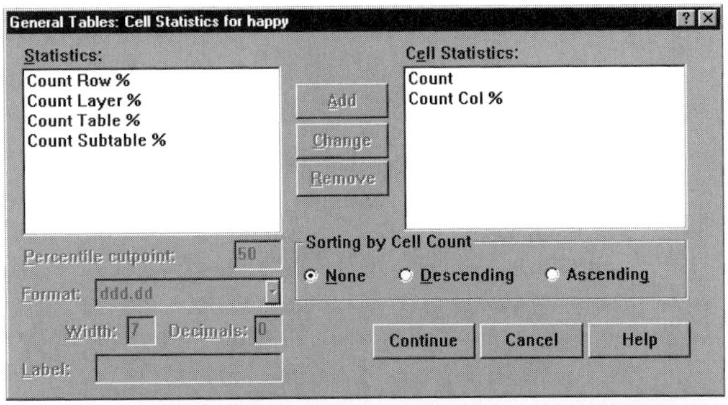

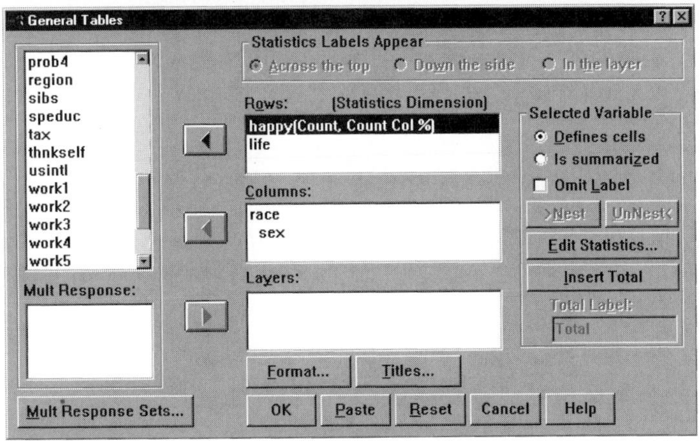

			Race of Respondent					
			White		Black		Other	
			Respondent's Sex		Respondent's Sex		Respondent's Sex	
			Male	Female	Male	Female	Male	Female
General Happiness	Very Happy	Count	180	229	19	27	7	5
		Col %	33.1%	32.1%	27.1%	20.6%	35.0%	18.5%
	Pretty Happy	Count	326	404	38	78	10	16
		Col %	60.0%	56.7%	54.3%	59.5%	50.0%	59.3%
	Not Too Happy	Count	37	80	13	26	3	6
		Col %	6.8%	11.2%	18.6%	19.8%	15.0%	22.2%
Is Life Exciting or Dull	Exciting		181	190	25	26	7	5
	Routine		173	240	20	49	7	16
	Dull		11	23	1	5		1

Even though *happy* is a variable in the rows, the percentage assigned to it is a column percentage. This means that each column adds up to 100%. If you want percentages for *life* to be displayed in the rows as well, select *life*, and then click on Edit Statistics again. Since you have already selected statistics for one variable (*happy*), those statistics will appear on the Cell Statistics list by default. Because all of the variables in the rows now have the same statistics, the options under Statistics Labels Appear become enabled again. Select In the layer under Statistics Labels Appear. Click on OK to generate the table shown in Figure 9.9. Each statistic forms a separate layer, even though the statistics are assigned to row variables and the percentage is a column percentage.

Figure 9.9   Percentages for all variables in the rows

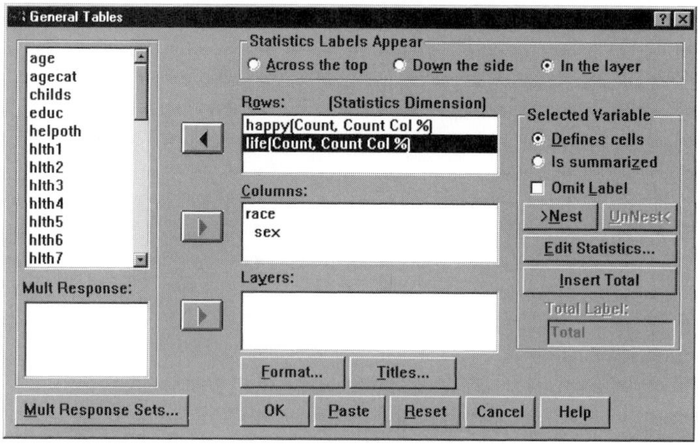

Figure 9.9   Percentages for all variables in the rows (Continued)

Count

		Race of Respondent					
		White		Black		Other	
		Respondent's Sex		Respondent's Sex		Respondent's Sex	
		Male	Female	Male	Female	Male	Female
General Happiness	Very Happy	180	229	19	27	7	5
	Pretty Happy	326	404	38	78	10	16
	Not Too Happy	37	80	13	26	3	6
Is Life Exciting or Dull	Exciting	181	190	25	26	7	5
	Routine	173	240	20	49	7	16
	Dull	11	23	1	5		1

Col %

		Race of Respondent					
		White		Black		Other	
		Respondent's Sex		Respondent's Sex		Respondent's Sex	
		Male	Female	Male	Female	Male	Female
General Happiness	Very Happy	33.1%	32.1%	27.1%	20.6%	35.0%	18.5%
	Pretty Happy	60.0%	56.7%	54.3%	59.5%	50.0%	59.3%
	Not Too Happy	6.8%	11.2%	18.6%	19.8%	15.0%	22.2%
Is Life Exciting or Dull	Exciting	49.6%	41.9%	54.3%	32.5%	50.0%	22.7%
	Routine	47.4%	53.0%	43.5%	61.3%	50.0%	72.7%
	Dull	3.0%	5.1%	2.2%	6.3%		4.5%

The Statistics Dimension

When you select percentages for a variable, you may notice the words Statistics Dimension in parentheses. Statistics can be assigned only to variables in the same dimension. That dimension is called the **statistics dimension**. For the table in Figure 9.9, the statistics dimension is the rows because the variables to which statistics are assigned (*happy* and *life*) are in the rows. The statistics dimension does not affect the kind of percentages that can be assigned. For example, in Figure 9.9, column percentages are calculated, even though the statistics dimension is the rows. If all variables in the table have the same statistics, the statistics dimension does not affect where the statistics labels are placed either. In Figure 9.9, statistics are displayed in the layers dimension, even though the statistics dimension is the rows. The statistics dimension refers only to the dimension in which statistics are assigned.

To change the statistics dimension, first clear all statistics assigned to variables in that dimension. You can clear the statistics from all of the variables on a list by moving them all to the source variable list and then back to the dimension list. Do this for *happy* and *life*. The words Statistics Dimension no longer appear in the dialog box. You can now assign statistics in any dimension you want. The table in Figure 9.10 shows *happy* and *life* stacked in the rows and *race* and *sex* stacked in the columns. Counts and column percentages are assigned to *sex*.

Figure 9.10   Statistics dimension as columns

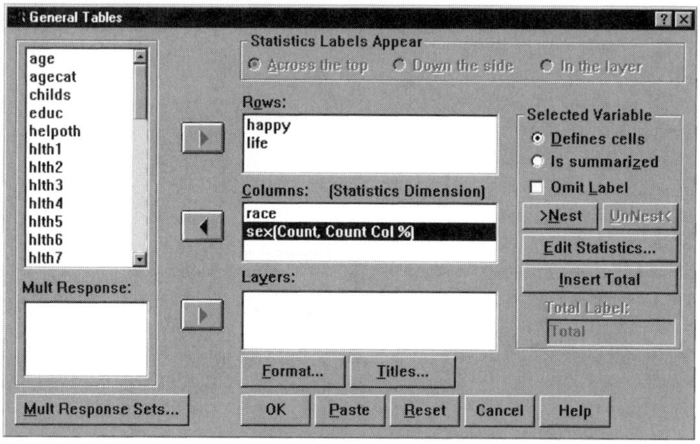

		Race of Respondent			Respondent's Sex			
					Male		Female	
		White	Black	Other	Count	Col %	Count	Col %
General Happiness	Very Happy	409	46	12	206	32.5%	261	30.0%
	Pretty Happy	730	116	26	374	59.1%	498	57.2%
	Not Too Happy	117	39	9	53	8.4%	112	12.9%
Is Life Exciting or Dull	Exciting	371	51	12	213	50.1%	221	39.8%
	Routine	413	69	23	200	47.1%	305	55.0%
	Dull	34	6	1	12	2.8%	29	5.2%

Because *sex* and *race* have different statistics and both variables are stacked in the columns, statistics labels are displayed in the columns.

Nesting with Different Statistics

In Figure 9.10, *sex* and *race* have different statistics and are stacked in the same dimension. This forces the statistics labels into that dimension. If *sex* is nested under *race*, as shown in Figure 9.9, the statistics labels are placed in the dimension specified by the option selected under Statistics Labels Appear. Figure 9.11 shows *happy* and *life* stacked in the rows and *sex* nested under *race* in the columns. Counts and column percentages are assigned to *sex*.

Figure 9.11   Nesting with different statistics

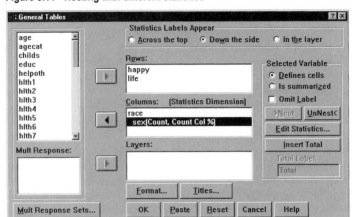

			Race of Respondent					
			White		Black		Other	
			Respondent's Sex		Respondent's Sex		Respondent's Sex	
			Male	Female	Male	Female	Male	Female
General Happiness	Very Happy	Count	180	229	19	27	7	5
		Col %	33.1%	32.1%	27.1%	20.6%	35.0%	18.5%
	Pretty Happy	Count	326	404	38	78	10	16
		Col %	60.0%	56.7%	54.3%	59.5%	50.0%	59.3%
	Not Too Happy	Count	37	80	13	26	3	6
		Col %	6.8%	11.2%	18.6%	19.8%	15.0%	22.2%
Is Life Exciting or Dull	Exciting	Count	181	190	25	26	7	5
		Col %	49.6%	41.9%	54.3%	32.5%	50.0%	22.7%
	Routine	Count	173	240	20	49	7	16
		Col %	47.4%	53.0%	43.5%	61.3%	50.0%	72.7%
	Dull	Count	11	23	1	5		1
		Col %	3.0%	5.1%	2.2%	6.3%		4.5%

While you can always assign statistics to variables at the lowest level of nesting, statistics cannot be assigned to controlling variables. For example, in Figure 9.11, statistics cannot be assigned to *race*.

10 Summary Statistics in General Tables

The Basic Tables procedure can be used to obtain summary statistics, but different statistics cannot be assigned to different variables. This chapter describes how to use summary statistics with the General Tables procedure. The chapter introduces several simple tables that request summary variables, which can be produced with either the Basic Tables or the General Tables procedure. Once the basics are explained, tables that can be produced only with the General Tables procedure are described in more detail.

Summarizing Variables with Means

Any noncategorical variable in a table should be summarized. To summarize a variable, select the variable and click on Is summarized under Selected Variable in the General Tables dialog box. By default, the mean of a summarized variable will be shown in the table.

For example, the dialog box in Figure 10.1 shows the mean for the variables for age, level of education, number of siblings, and number of children. Notice the (S) beside each variable in the dialog box. This indicates that they are summarized.

Figure 10.1   Summarized variable

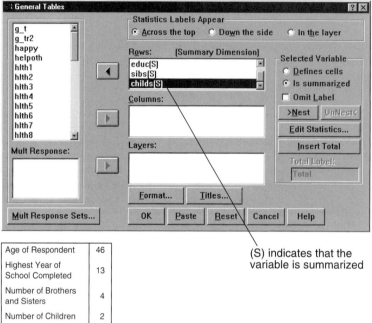

(S) indicates that the
variable is summarized

Age of Respondent	46
Highest Year of School Completed	13
Number of Brothers and Sisters	4
Number of Children	2

Summary variables can be summarized within cells determined by the values of category variables. For example, Figure 10.2 shows the *age* and *educ* variables summarized in the columns with value labels for *region* and *happy* stacked in the rows.

Figure 10.2   Summary variables broken into categories

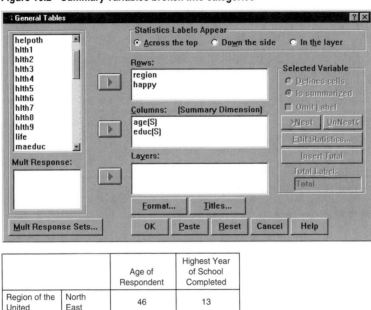

		Age of Respondent	Highest Year of School Completed
Region of the United States	North East	46	13
	South East	48	12
	West	44	13
General Happiness	Very Happy	47	13
	Pretty Happy	45	13
	Not Too Happy	46	12

Changing the Summary Dimension

In the last example, *age* and *educ* are in the columns. In the Columns list in the dialog box, notice the words Summary Dimension in parentheses. The dimension that contains summarized variables is called the **summary dimension**. Variables can be summarized only in the summary dimension. To change the summary dimension, move the summarized variables back to the source variable list (or select them and click on Defines cells). For example, move *age* and *educ* back to the source variable list. Now you can summarize a variable in any dimension. To summarize *age* and *educ* in the layers dimension, for example, move *sex* into the columns dimension and *age* and *educ* into the layers dimension. Select *age* and click on Is summarized. Repeat the process for *educ*. Notice that the summary dimension has changed from the columns dimension to the layers dimension. The resulting table and the dialog box that generated it are shown in Figure 10.3.

Figure 10.3   Summary variables in the layers dimension

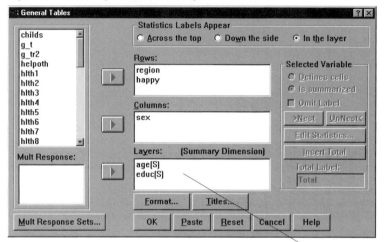

Age of Respondent

		Respondent's Sex	
		Male	Female
Region of the United States	North East	44	47
	South East	46	49
	West	43	44
General Happiness	Very Happy	47	47
	Pretty Happy	43	46
	Not Too Happy	44	47

(Summary Dimension) indicates that variables can be summarized in this dimension

Highest Year of School Completed

		Respondent's Sex	
		Male	Female
Region of the United States	North East	13	13
	South East	13	12
	West	13	13
General Happiness	Very Happy	14	13
	Pretty Happy	13	13
	Not Too Happy	12	12

Nesting with Means

You may want to combine the two layers of information shown in Figure 10.3—age and level of education—into a single layer. As discussed in Chapter 2, nesting collapses dimensions. While you cannot nest one summarized variable beneath another, you can nest summary variables beneath category variables. In Figure 10.4, the summary variables *age* and *educ* are nested beneath the category variable *sex*.

Figure 10.4   Nested summary variables

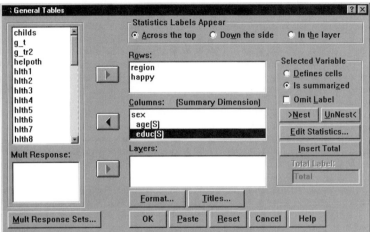

		Respondent's Sex			
		Male		Female	
		Age of Respondent	Highest Year of School Completed	Age of Respondent	Highest Year of School Completed
Region of the United States	North East	44	13	47	13
	South East	46	13	49	12
	West	43	13	44	13
General Happiness	Very Happy	47	14	47	13
	Pretty Happy	43	13	46	13
	Not Too Happy	44	12	47	12

In a general table, a variable cannot be nested beneath a summary variable. The summary variable must always be at the lowest level of nesting.

You can achieve the same effect by using the Pivot Table Editor on the table illustrated in Figure 10.3. Move the layer icon from the layer dimension to the column dimension.

Valid Number of Cases

To display the number of valid (nonmissing) cases along with the mean, select a variable in the summary dimension and click on Edit Statistics to open the General Tables Cell Statistics dialog box. Move Valid Value Count to the Cell Statistics list by selecting it and clicking on Add. When you return to the General Tables dialog box, notice that the words Summary Dimension have changed to Summary & Statistics. In the example shown in Figure 10.5, this means that both the summary and statistics dimensions are now in the columns dimension. (It is possible to separate the statistics and summary dimensions, but this is not a good practice because the table becomes difficult to interpret. To get a statistics dimension that is different from the summary dimension, select variables in one dimension and make them summary variables by clicking on Is summarized, but do not edit statistics. Select variables in another dimension and edit statistics. You may assign counts or percentages to those variables.) The table with both the valid value count and the mean for *age* but only the mean for *educ* is shown in Figure 10.5. This table can be produced only with the General Tables procedure.

Figure 10.5   Different statistics for different summary variables

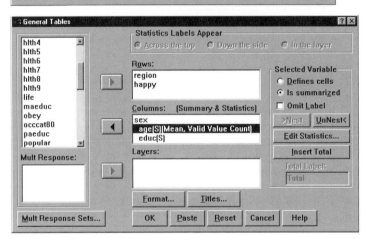

		Respondent's Sex				
		Male			Female	
		Age of Respondent		Highest Year of School Completed	Age of Respondent		Highest Year of School Completed
		Mean	Valid N	Completed	Mean	Valid N	Completed
Region of the United States	North East	44	N=281	13	47	N=396	13
	South East	46	N=177	13	49	N=237	12
	West	43	N=178	13	44	N=245	13
General Happiness	Very Happy	47	N=206	14	47	N=261	13
	Pretty Happy	43	N=374	13	46	N=497	13
	Not Too Happy	44	N=53	12	47	N=111	12

Other Summary Statistics

If you want other summary statistics, such as the standard deviation and range, select them from the General Tables Cell Statistics dialog box for each variable to which you want them to apply. For example, the table in Figure 10.6 shows the range and standard deviation applied to *age* and *educ*.

Figure 10.6   Other summary statistics

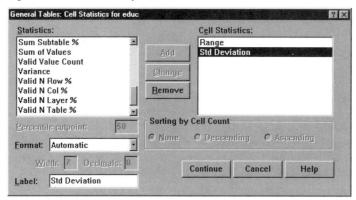

		Respondent's Sex						
		Male				Female		
		Age of Respondent		Highest Year of School Completed		Age of Respondent		Highest Year of School Completed	
		Range	Std Deviation	Range	Std Deviation	Range	Std Deviation	Range	Std Deviation
Region of the United States	North East	70	17	17	3	71	18	15	3
	South East	63	17	17	3	71	19	20	3
	West	67	17	16	3	70	18	17	3
General Happiness	Very Happy	62	17	17	3	70	19	20	3
	Pretty Happy	71	17	17	3	71	18	20	3
	Not Too Happy	63	17	16	3	69	18	15	3

If you want to change a statistic label or the format, width, or number of decimals for a statistic, select the statistic on the Cell Statistics list. After you edit the attributes, click on Change, and then click on Continue to return to the main dialog box. Figure 10.7 shows the table in Figure 10.6 with the label attribute modified for standard deviation.

Figure 10.7   Modified label attribute for standard deviation

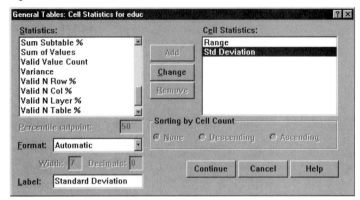

		Respondent's Sex						
		Male				Female		
		Age of Respondent		Highest Year of School Completed		Age of Respondent		Highest Year of School Completed	
		Range	Standard Deviation	Range	Standard Deviation	Range	Standard Deviation	Range	Standard Deviation
Region of the United States	North East	70	17	17	3	71	18	15	3
	South East	63	17	17	3	71	19	20	3
	West	67	17	16	3	70	18	17	3
General Happiness	Very Happy	62	17	17	3	70	19	20	3
	Pretty Happy	71	17	17	3	71	18	20	3
	Not Too Happy	63	17	16	3	69	18	15	3

11 Totals in General Tables

The Basic Tables procedure can be used to get totals, but is not nearly as flexible as the General Tables procedure. This chapter introduces the various kinds of totals that can be obtained with General Tables.

Simple Totals

To get simple totals with the General Tables procedure, select the category variable you want to total and click on Insert Total in the General Tables main dialog box. A total for the selected variable appears in the dialog box. For example, move *happy* to the Rows list and *region* to the Columns list. Select *happy* and click on Insert Total. A new variable, called *happyTotal*, appears in the Rows list below *happy*. Select *region* and click on Insert Total again. Another variable, called *regionTotal*, appears in the Columns list below *region*. The generated table appears in Figure 11.1.

Figure 11.1   Simple totals

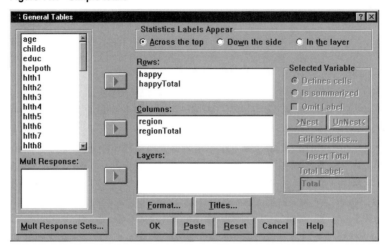

		Region of the United States			
		North East	South East	West	**Total**
General Happiness	Very Happy	185	149	133	**467**
	Pretty Happy	412	215	245	**872**
	Not Too Happy	76	47	42	**165**
Total		**673**	**411**	**420**	**1504**

By default, a total will give the same statistic as the variable totaled. For example, in the table in Figure 11.2, since counts and column percentages are assigned to *happy*, the total of *happy* also gives counts and column percentages.

Figure 11.2   Total of counts and column percentages

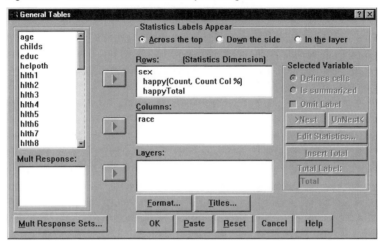

				Race of Respondent					
				White		Black		Other	
				Count	Col %	Count	Col %	Count	Col %
Respondent's Sex	Male	General Happiness	Very Happy	180	14.3%	19	9.5%	7	14.9%
			Pretty Happy	326	26.0%	38	18.9%	10	21.3%
			Not Too Happy	37	2.9%	13	6.5%	3	6.4%
		Total		**543**	**43.2%**	**70**	**34.8%**	**20**	**42.6%**
	Female	General Happiness	Very Happy	229	18.2%	27	13.4%	5	10.6%
			Pretty Happy	404	32.2%	78	38.8%	16	34.0%
			Not Too Happy	80	6.4%	26	12.9%	6	12.8%
		Total		**713**	**56.8%**	**131**	**65.2%**	**27**	**57.4%**

You can total any variable in the table except another total, a summary variable, or a variable nested under a variable that is totaled. In the previous example, you can total *sex* or *happy*, but not both.

Totals of Summary Variables

You cannot total across summary variables, but when one or more summary variables are nested under a category variable, you can total the summary variables across the cells defined by the category variable. You assign the total to the category variable. For example, nest *age* and *educ* under *sex* in the rows. Select Is summarized for *age* and *educ*. Then select *sex* and click on Insert Total. The resulting table is shown in Figure 11.3.

Figure 11.3   Total of summary variables

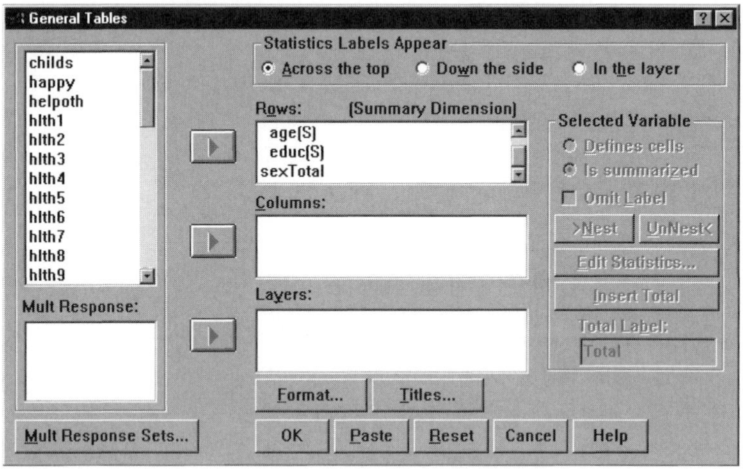

Respondent's Sex	Male	Age of Respondent	44
		Highest Year of School Completed	13
	Female	Age of Respondent	47
		Highest Year of School Completed	13
Total	**Age of Respondent**		**46**
	Highest Year of School Completed		**13**

Notice that the total for *sex* shows totals for both of the variables nested under sex. Each variable shown for the total has the same statistics as the variables totaled.

Totals with Different Statistics

Sometimes you will want a different statistic for a total than for the variable it totals. For example, in Figure 11.4, the total of column percentages does not provide much useful information.

Figure 11.4   Default total

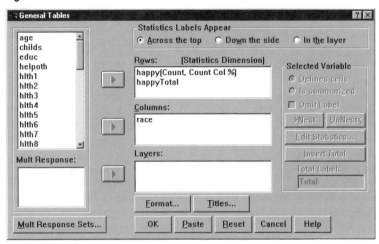

		Race of Respondent					
		White		Black		Other	
		Count	Col %	Count	Col %	Count	Col %
General Happiness	Very Happy	409	32.6%	46	22.9%	12	25.5%
	Pretty Happy	730	58.1%	116	57.7%	26	55.3%
	Not Too Happy	117	9.3%	39	19.4%	9	19.1%
Total		**1256**	**100.0%**	**201**	**100.0%**	**47**	**100.0%**

To get total counts only, select *happyTotal* and click on Edit Statistics to open the General Tables Total Statistics dialog box, as shown in Figure 11.5.

Figure 11.5   General Tables Total Statistics dialog box

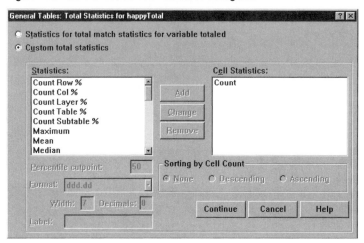

Select Custom total statistics. Add Count to the Cell Statistics list and click on Continue. Since different statistics have been selected for different variables in the rows, the statistics labels are automatically displayed in the rows. The resulting table is shown in Figure 11.6.

Figure 11.6   Custom statistics for total

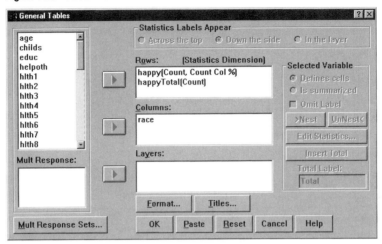

			Race of Respondent		
			White	Black	Other
General Happiness	Very Happy	Count	409	46	12
		Col %	32.6%	22.9%	25.5%
	Pretty Happy	Count	730	116	26
		Col %	58.1%	57.7%	55.3%
	Not Too Happy	Count	117	39	9
		Col %	9.3%	19.4%	19.1%
Total	**Count**		**1256**	**201**	**47**

Grand Totals

To create a **grand total** (a total of a number of totals), it is necessary to create a **dummy variable**—a variable with a value of 1 for all valid cases. To create a dummy variable, from the menus choose:

Transform
  Compute...

This opens the Compute Variable dialog box. Assign a name to your dummy variable. Enter the variable name in the Target Variable text box and type 1 in the Numeric Expression list to assign the dummy variable a value of 1. To make the dummy variable valid for valid cases only, click on If to open the Compute Variable If Cases dialog box. Click on Include if case satisfies condition, and enter the condition and name of the variable for which you want the grand total, as in

`~missing(happy)`

If the variable is nested, follow the parentheses with an "and" symbol (&) and repeat the process for the controlling variable. If that variable is nested, repeat the same process.

For example, if you want a grand total of *happy* nested beneath *sex*, the condition should read `~missing(happy) & ~missing(sex)`. Click on Continue. The expression you entered will appear after If, as shown in Figure 11.7. Click on OK. This creates a new variable that has a value of 1 for all valid cases of *happy* and *sex*. From the Data Editor, give the variable a value label of *Grand Total* for the value 1. This variable can be used to create a total of a number of totals.

Figure 11.7   Compute grand total variable

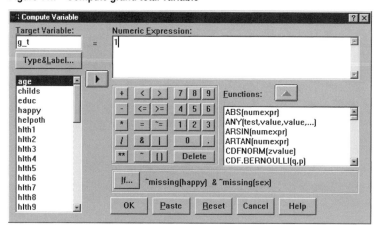

Figure 11.8 shows a table with *happy* nested under *sex* in the rows and *region* in the columns. The table shows a simple total and a grand total. Notice that Omit Label is selected for the dummy variable.

Figure 11.8   Grand total

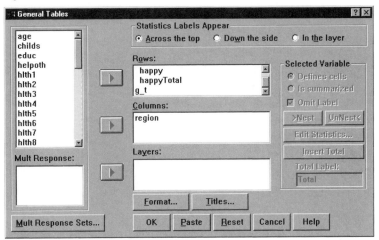

				Region of the United States		
				North East	South East	West
Respondent's Sex	Male	General Happiness	Very Happy	78	70	58
			Pretty Happy	176	94	104
			Not Too Happy	26	12	15
		Total		**280**	**176**	**177**
	Female	General Happiness	Very Happy	107	79	75
			Pretty Happy	236	121	141
			Not Too Happy	50	35	27
		Total		**393**	**235**	**243**
Grand Total				**673**	**411**	**420**

If the variables for which you want a grand total are stacked, create a separate grand total for each of the stacked variables. For example, Figure 11.9 shows a table with *happy* nested under *race*, which is stacked with *life* nested under *sex*. *Happy*, *race*, *sex*, and *life* are in the rows and *region* is in the columns. The "if" statement for the grand total of *happy* and *race* is ~missing(happy) & ~missing(race). The "if" statement for the grand total of *life* and *sex* is ~missing(life) & ~missing(sex). The variable labels for *happy* and *life* are omitted to conserve space.

Figure 11.9   Grand totals with stacking

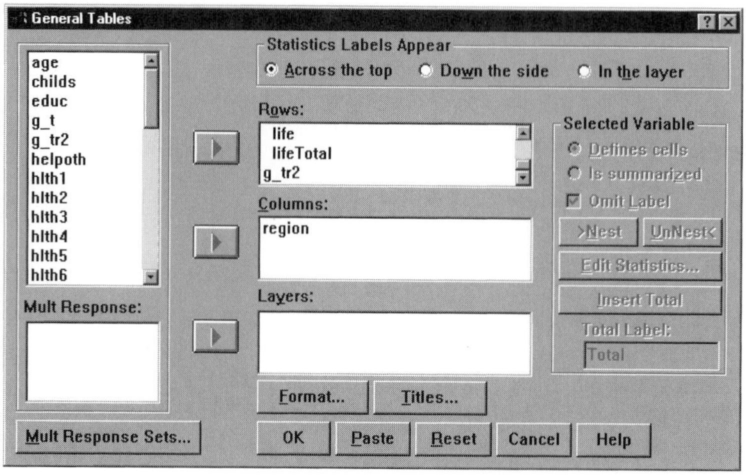

			Region of the United States		
			North East	South East	West
Race of Respondent	White	Very Happy	162	123	124
		Pretty Happy	361	150	219
		Not Too Happy	55	31	31
		Total	**578**	**304**	**374**
	Black	Very Happy	18	23	5
		Pretty Happy	44	56	16
		Not Too Happy	19	14	6
		Total	**81**	**93**	**27**
	Other	Very Happy	5	3	4
		Pretty Happy	7	9	10
		Not Too Happy	2	2	5
		Total	**14**	**14**	**19**
Grand Total			**673**	**411**	**420**
Respondent's Sex	Male	Exciting	92	56	65
		Routine	88	58	54
		Dull	7	3	2
		Total	187	117	121
	Female	Exciting	94	51	76
		Routine	140	90	75
		Dull	12	9	8
		Total	**246**	**150**	**159**
Grand Total			**433**	**267**	**280**

Dialog Box Reference

Dialog Box Reference

There are four main custom tables dialog boxes: Basic Tables, General Tables, Multiple Response Tables, and Tables of Frequencies. Use Basic Tables for most tables. A Basic Table can contain summary variables and category variables. Use General Tables for tables that require different statistics for different variables, mixed nesting and stacking, or complex totals. Use Multiple Response Tables for basic tables that include multiple-response sets, and General Tables for more complex tables that include multiple-response sets; you can define multiple-response sets within either procedure. Use Tables of Frequencies for specialized tables that contain multiple variables with the same categories.

Basic Tables

Basic Tables produces publication-quality tables displaying crosstabulations and subgroup statistics. The selected summary variables are summarized in cells defined by the subgroup variables. The same statistics are reported for all variables summarized in the table. The default statistic displayed is the mean. If there are no summary variables, counts are displayed.

By default, summary variable labels or names are displayed down the left side of the table. You can define cells to display subgroups of cases in any combination of:

- Down the page (as separate rows).
- Across the page (as separate columns). The combination of **Down** and **Across** generates a crosstabular display.
- Spread across Separate Tables. Variables on this list subdivide the table into layers or groups of layers. Only one layer of the table is visible at a time. You can view other layers after the table is displayed in the Viewer by double-clicking the table and clicking the arrows on the layer pivot icon.

When multiple variables are on a subgroups list, you can nest the variables within each list or stack each variable separately. Nesting means that categories of one variable are shown under each category of the previous variable. Stacking displays categories of each variable as a block. Stacking can be thought of as taking separate tables and pasting them together into the same display.

To Obtain a Basic Table

▶ From the menus choose:

Statistics
  Custom Tables
    Basic Tables...

Figure 1   Basic Tables dialog box

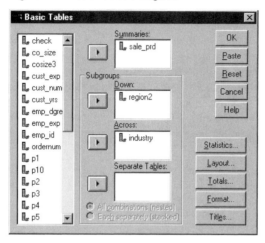

▶ Select one or more summary or subgroup variables. (At a minimum, you need only one variable in any one of these boxes.)

▶ Click Statistics to specify the statistics in the table.

▶ If you specify more than one grouping variable in any one dimension, you can choose between All combinations [nested] and Each separately [stacked].

You can also specify the layout for labels and nesting of variables, add titles, obtain totals over each group variable, and specify the format for empty cells and missing values.

Basic Tables Statistics

Different statistics are appropriate depending on whether you have selected summary variables or subgroup variables. Statistics for categorical variables include counts and percentages for different parts of the table. Statistics for summary variables include standard measures of central tendency and variability, plus percentiles, sums, and sum and valid case percentages for different dimensions in the table.

If no statistics are selected, the default is mean for tables with summary variables and counts for tables with no summary variables.

Figure 2   Basic Tables Statistics dialog box

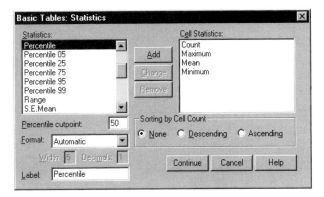

Cell Statistics. Lists the statistics that will be displayed in the table. Statistics specified here apply to the entire table. You can add and remove statistics from the list or change the format for a statistic after you have selected it.

Format and Label. You can choose a display format, width, number of decimals, and label for each statistic. Available formats include standard decimal, percentage, and currency formats. The currently selected formats are applied to statistics as you add them to the Cell Statistics list. You can also change the format for a statistic after you have added it to the list.

Sorting by Cell Count. Rearranges the cells within each row, column, or layer in the table according to the cell counts.

Search for "Basic Tables" in the online Help system for a complete list of available statistics.

Basic Tables Layout

Figure 3   Basic Tables Layout dialog box

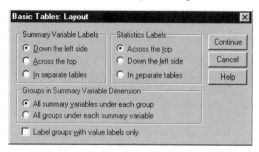

Summary Variable Labels. You can select the dimension in which you want the summary variable labels. If there are no summary variables, these options are disabled.

Statistics Labels. You can select the dimension in which you want the statistics labels displayed.

Groups in Summary Variable Dimension. If the summary variables are in the same dimension as subgroup variables, either the summary variables can be nested beneath each category of the subgroup variable, or the subgroup variable can be nested under each summary variable.

Label groups with value labels only. Eliminates the subgroup variable labels from the table. The categories are still identified by the value labels or values.

Basic Tables Totals

Figure 4   Basic Tables Totals dialog box

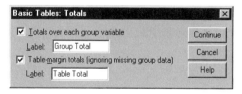

Totals can be added to tables that contain a subgroup variable. There are two kinds of totals:

- **Totals over each group variable.** In a table where subgroups are stacked, the total of each subgroup is reported after the subgroup variable. In a table where subgroups are nested, the total of the lowest-level subgroup is reported after the last nested variable in each category of the previous variable on the same list. Missing cases are not included in the total.

- **Table-margin totals (ignoring missing group data).** For each dimension in which there is a subgroup variable, a total is reported. The total summarizes across the whole table. For example, if the total is for rows, it summarizes all the rows in each column. Unlike other totals, missing cases of a subgroup variable are included in a table total of that variable. Missing cases of a summary variable are not included in a table total of the summary variable.

Table Format

Figure 5   Basic Tables Format dialog box

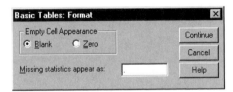

Empty Cell Appearance. Empty cells can either be left blank or display a zero.

Missing statistics appear as. Specify the character(s) to be used to represent missing values. The specification cannot be longer than 10 characters.

Table Titles

Figure 6   Basic Tables Titles dialog box

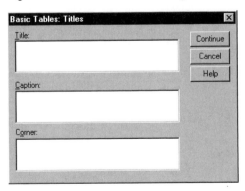

Title. The title is displayed above each table. You can specify up to 10 lines of text. By default, a single line is left blank between the table and the title. (This blank space can be adjusted on the Table Properties Cell Formats tab on the Format menu in the Pivot Table Editor.)

Caption. The caption is displayed under each table. The caption could be viewed as a footnote for the whole table. Footnotes for specific labels or data can be added from the View menu in the Data Editor.

)DATE keyword. Where)DATE is specified on a title or caption line, the current system date is printed. The date takes up nine characters.

Corner. You can specify up to 10 lines of text to be displayed in the upper left corner of the table where the space for the row titles meets the space for the column titles. Each line must fit within the row title column width. If you specify more lines than are available in the corner, the Viewer will print as many lines as will fit, starting with the first line specified.

• If any lines exceed the row title column width, the procedure issues an error message instead of producing a table.

• If the default TableLook uses the corner format, which reserves the corner for dimension labels in the rows, text specified in the dialog box will not appear in the Viewer. To view text in the corner, you must have Row Dimension Labels set as Nested in the Table Properties dialog box on the Format menu in the Pivot Table Editor. Notice that this option may be preset in the default TableLook.

General Tables

General Tables produces publication-quality tables displaying crosstabulations and sub-group statistics. You can produce tables showing different statistics for different variables, multiple-response variables, mixed nesting and stacking, or complex totals.

• Under most circumstances, you must select a row variable. You can also select one or more variables to define columns or layers. For example, to produce a simple crosstabulation, select one variable to define rows and one variable to define columns. If you have a layer variable, you must also have a row variable and a column variable.

• For each selected variable, you can specify whether the variable is a grouping variable used to define cells or a summary variable for which statistics are displayed in the table. You can also specify different statistics for each variable. If more than one variable is selected for a given dimension, you can specify whether the variables should be stacked or nested within the dimension.

Layering is a method of fitting a third dimension into a two-dimensional display. Only one layer of the table is visible at a time. You can view other layers after the table is displayed in the Viewer by double-clicking the table and clicking the arrows on the layer pivot icon.

Most tables that display the same summary statistic(s) for each variable can be obtained more easily with the Basic Tables procedure. Most basic tables that include multiple-response sets can be obtained more easily with the Multiple Response Tables procedure. Side-by-side frequency tables are readily available from the Tables of Frequencies procedure.

Statistics Labels Appear. You can display statistics across the top (in columns), down the side (in rows), or in separate layers. Descriptive statistics labels are used as headings in the selected dimension. If statistics labels appear across the top, a variable need not be in the columns for a variable to be placed in the layers. If statistics labels appear down the side, a variable need not be in the rows for a variable to be placed in the columns.

Selected Variable. For each variable that you select, you can specify whether the variable is a grouping variable used to define cells or a summary variable for which statistics are displayed in the table. Variables that define cells should have distinct categories (such as sex or religion). The statistics associated with a variable that defines cells are counts and percentages. The first summary variable you specify defines the summary dimension. The words "Summary Dimension" appear above the variable list for that dimension, and you cannot summarize variables in another dimension.

- **Nest.** You can nest the selected variable to the previous variable on the same dimension list. Nesting is a way to compress two dimensions into a single dimension or a way to break summary variables into categories. A variable can be nested only one level beneath the previous variable. You can also un-nest a variable that has been nested.

- **Edit Statistics.** Statistics selected here apply only to the selected variable. The first time you edit statistics for a variable, you define the statistics dimension. The words "Statistics Dimension" appear next to the dimension title, and you can subsequently edit statistics only in that dimension.

- **Insert Total.** Inserts a total variable after the selected variable. The new variable has the name *variableTotal*, where *variable* is the name of the selected variable. You cannot total another total or total a variable that has a total nested beneath it. You can edit statistics or summarize a total just like a normal variable.

Mult Response. Lists currently defined multiple-response sets. You can click Mult Response Sets to define a new set.

To Obtain a General Table

▶   From the menus choose:

Statistics
  Custom Tables
    General Tables...

Figure 7   General Tables dialog box

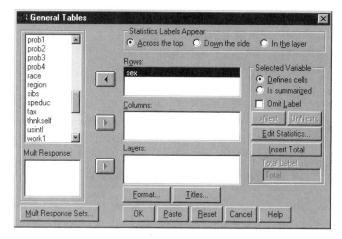

▶   Select one or more row variables.*

▶   Optionally select one or more variables to define columns or layers.

▶   Click any selected variable to change its function or edit statistics for the variable.

* The minimum specifications depend on the dimension in which statistics labels appear. You must select a row variable unless you select Down the side in the Statistics Labels Appear group at the top of the dialog box.

General Tables Cell Statistics

The statistics available depend on whether the selected variable is a grouping variable, summary variable, multiple-response set, or total. Statistics for categorical variables include counts and percentages for different parts of the table. Statistics for summary variables include standard measures of central tendency and variability, percentiles, sums, and sum and valid case percentages for different dimensions in the table. For multiple-response sets, you can choose counts, responses, respondents, or response percentages. The default statistic is counts for grouping variables and mean for summary variables.

Figure 8   Cell statistics for a category variable

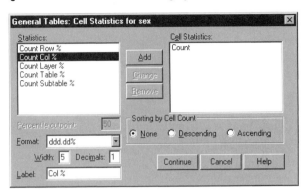

Cell Statistics. Lists the statistics that will be displayed in the table. Statistics specified here apply to the entire table. You can add and remove statistics from the list or change the format for a statistic after you have selected it.

Format and Label. You can choose a display format, width, number of decimals, and label for each statistic. Available formats include standard decimal, percentage, and currency formats. The currently selected formats are applied to statistics as you add them to the Cell Statistics list. You can also change the format for a statistic after you have added it to the list.

Sorting by Cell Count. Rearranges the cells within each row, column, or layer in the table according to the cell counts.

Figure 9   Cell statistics for a summary variable

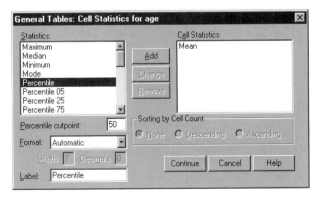

Figure 10   Cell statistics for a multiple-response set

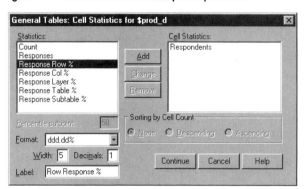

Figure 11   Cell statistics for totals

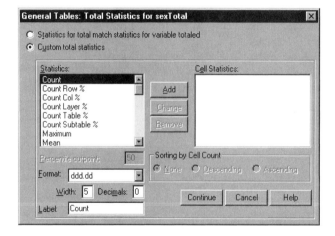

For totals, the following options are available:

- **Statistics for total match statistics for variable totaled.** This is the default. Under most circumstances, this produces the clearest tables.

- **Custom total statistics.** If you choose this option, move the statistics you want reported for the total from the Statistics list to the Cell Statistics list. The statistics available for most totals include the statistics available for variables that define cells and those available for variables that are summarized. The statistics available for totals of multiple-response sets are the same as those available for the multiple-response set.

Search for "General Tables" in the online Help system for a complete list of available statistics.

Note: The Format and Titles dialog boxes for General Tables are the same as described for Basic Tables.

General Tables Define Multiple-Response Sets

See "Multiple Response Tables: Define Multiple-Response Sets" on p. 142 for information on defining multiple-response sets.

Multiple Response Tables

Multiple Response Tables produces basic frequency and crosstabulation tables in which one or more of the variables is a multiple response set. You are not required to have a multiple response set defined to use this procedure, but you may obtain better results with Basic Tables if you do not need to use a multiple response set.

To create a table, you must place at least one variable or multiple response set in at least one of the three table dimensions.

Multiple Response Sets. Lists currently defined multiple-response sets. You can click Define Sets to define a new set.

Nesting. If you specify more than one variable in any one dimension, you can choose whether to nest each lower variable within categories of the variable above it on the list. Nesting produces cells for all combinations of the nested variable within the nesting variable. If Nesting is not selected for a dimension, logically separate but physically connected (concatenated) tables are produced for each variable.

To Obtain a Multiple Response Table

▶   From the menus choose:

Statistics
  Custom Tables
    Multiple Response Tables...

Figure 12   Multiple Response Tables dialog box

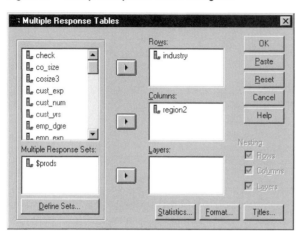

▶ If you do not have any multiple response sets defined, click Define Sets and define one. Select the variables that make up the set and indicate whether these variables are coded as dichotomies or categories (if dichotomies, indicate what value is to be counted). Assign a name and optionally a label to the set, click Add to add it to the list and Save when you have defined all the sets you want.

▶ Select a variable or multiple response sets for one of the table dimensions.

▶ Optionally, select one or more variables or multiple response sets to define other dimensions.

Multiple Response Tables: Define Multiple-Response Sets

Multiple Response allows you to specify the variables making up a multiple-response or multiple-dichotomy set for use in multiple-response frequency tables or crosstabulations. Multiple-response sets use multiple variables to record responses to questions where the respondent can give more than one answer. For example, "Which of the following magazines do you read regularly?" is a multiple-response question. Sets defined within the Tables procedure are saved when you save your data file; these sets can be used in later sessions that access that data file.

Figure 13   Multiple Response Tables Define Multiple-Response Sets dialog box

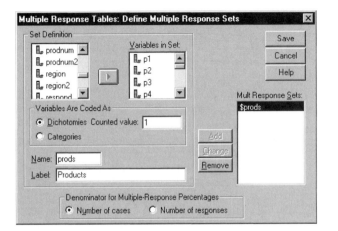

Variables in Set. Displays the variables to be included in the multiple-response set.

Variables Are Coded As. Before defining a multiple-response set, you must know how your data were coded. If each category (each magazine, for example) is coded as a separate variable, the multiple-response set is coded as dichotomies. In this case, each variable in the set has a value that indicates that the respondent checked this selection ;any other value indicates that the respondent did not check this selection.

The other strategy for coding multiple-response variables is most useful when there are many possible responses but each respondent is expected to select just a few. For example, if there are 100 magazines on the list and each person is expected to select five magazines, the data might be coded as five variables that can each take on one of 100 different values.

Name and Label. You must specify a name for the multiple-response set. The name follows normal naming conventions, except that it can be no longer than seven characters. You can optionally specify a label.

Mult Response Sets. Displays the multiple-response sets that are defined. You can add, change, and remove sets from the list.

Denominator for Multiple-Response Percentages. Defines the denominator to be used for calculating cell percentages. You can calculate cell percentages based on the number of cases or the number of responses.

Tables of Frequencies

Tables of Frequencies allows you to produce specialized tables that contain multiple variables with the same values. By default, the variables form columns and the categories form rows. Each cell displays the number of cases in that category. Optionally, you can select one or more subgroup variables.

Frequencies for. By default, variables on this list are displayed with their variable labels across the top of the table and their value labels on the left side of the table. All variables on this list should have the same categories.

Subgroups. You can divide the table into columns within each table or into separate tables (layers). If you divide the table into columns, all variables are displayed for each subgroup. If you divide the table into separate layers, only one layer of the table is visible at a time. You can view other layers after the table is displayed in the Viewer by double-clicking the table and clicking the arrows on the layer pivot icon.

When multiple variables are on a Subgroups list, you nest or stack the variables on the list. If you select **All combinations [nested]**, each variable is nested under the previous variable on the same list. That is, the categories of one variable are shown under each category of the previous variable. If you select **Each separately [stacked]**, categories of each variable are shown as a block. Stacking can be thought of as taking separate tables and pasting them together into the same display.

To Obtain a Table of Frequencies

▶ From the menus choose:

Statistics
  Custom Tables
    Tables of Frequencies...

Figure 14   Tables of Frequencies dialog box

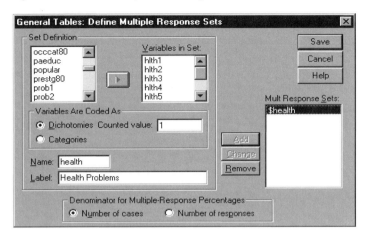

▶ Select one or more frequency variables.

▶ Optionally, you can select a subgroup variable to divide the table into separate columns or layers.

You can also request additional statistics, specify the layout for labels, and specify the format for empty cells and missing values.

Tables of Frequencies Statistics

Figure 15   Tables of Frequencies Statistics dialog box

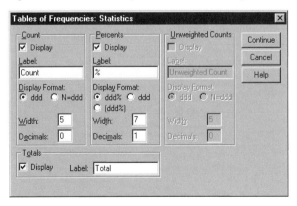

Statistics available include counts, percentages, and totals. You can specify a different label, display format, width, and number of decimals for each statistic that you choose to display.

If case weights are in effect, you can request unweighted counts.

Tables of Frequencies Layout

Figure 16   Tables of Frequencies Layout dialog box

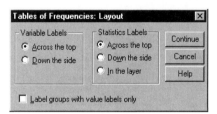

Tables of Frequencies Layout allows you to select the dimension in which variable and statistics labels are displayed.

Variable Labels. You can place frequency variable labels across the top (in columns) or down the side (in rows). If any subgroup variables have been selected in the Tables of Frequencies dialog box to display subgroups in each table, variable labels are nested under the values of the subgroup variables.

Statistics Labels. You can place statistics labels across the top, down the side, or in layers. If statistics are placed in layers, only one layer of the table is visible at a time. You can view other layers after the table is displayed in the Viewer by double-clicking the table and clicking the arrows on the layer pivot icon.

Label groups with value labels only. Eliminates the variable labels from the table for subgroup variables.

Note: The Format and Titles dialog boxes for Tables of Frequencies are the same as described for Basic Tables.

Syntax Reference

Introduction

This section of the Syntax Reference provides general information about the syntax in the Tables procedure. Following this introduction, a detailed section describes the subcommands individually in alphabetical order.

Syntax Notation

Like other commands, a TABLES command begins on a new line, is followed by subcommands and keywords, and ends with a period. A command, including its subcommands with related specifications, can continue for as many lines as needed. Syntax can be pasted from a dialog box by clicking on Paste, or it can be entered directly into a syntax window. To get a new syntax window, from the menus choose:

File
  New ▶
    Syntax...

This opens a new window in which you can enter syntax. To execute a single command, place the cursor somewhere in the command and from the menus choose:

Run
  Current

To execute multiple commands, drag the cursor across portions of all the commands. This highlights the section over which you drag the cursor. From the menus choose:

Run
  Selection

There are two other options for executing commands. Place the cursor (as described above) for a single command or multiple commands and click the Run tool on the toolbar or click the right mouse button and choose Run Current.

Like other commands, the following simple rules apply to the TABLES command:

- Subcommands are separated by slashes. The slash before the first subcommand on a command is optional.

- Keywords are not case sensitive, and three-letter abbreviations can be used for most keywords.

- Variable names must be spelled out in full.

- You can use as many lines as you want to specify a single command. However, text included within apostrophes or quotation marks must be contained on a single line.

- You can add space or break lines at almost any point where a single blank is allowed, such as around slashes, parentheses, table structure operators, or between variable names.

- Each line of syntax cannot exceed 80 characters.
- The period must be used as the decimal indicator.

The syntax for each subcommand on the TABLES command is presented in the subcommands section. The syntax diagrams there and elsewhere in this manual use a shorthand style that follows these rules:

- Elements printed in upper case are subcommands or keywords.
- Elements in lower case describe items you should provide.
- Subcommands and keywords can be truncated up to the first three characters; however, the statistical format names, such as COMMA, must be spelled out in full.
- Equals signs are optional.
- Special delimiters (:, (), =, ', /, and ") must be entered exactly as shown.
- Slashes are required between subcommands.
- Blanks or commas must separate keywords, names, labels, and numbers.
- Elements enclosed in square brackets [ ] are optional. Brackets are not part of the syntax.
- Braces { } are not part of the syntax either. They indicate a choice among the elements they enclose. Use only one alternative from a list in braces.
- Ellipses ... also are not part of the syntax. They indicate the option of repeating an element or an entire sequence of elements.
- Default options are in boldface type. A default is the option that TABLES assumes is in effect if you do not explicitly request an alternative.

Subcommand Types

The Tables procedure has two types of subcommands: global and local. **Global subcommands** affect all of the tables that a TABLES command produces. These subcommands can appear in any order but must precede the first TABLE subcommand. Global subcommands do things such as define how a variable is going to be used or define the format of the subsequent tables. **Local subcommands** include the TABLE subcommand itself and the subcommands that follow TABLE. They apply only to the table specified by the preceding TABLE subcommand. Local subcommands define what is going to be in a table and how it's going to be structured. Each TABLE subcommand on a TABLES command can have its own local subcommands. No matter how many TABLE subcommands are issued, the Tables procedure reads the data just once for the entire procedure.

Summary of TABLES Subcommands

Global subcommands (see Table 1) must precede the first TABLE subcommand. They apply to all tables created by a single TABLES command.

Table 1   Global subcommands

Subcommand	Explanation
AUTOLABEL	Creates labels for all tables
BASE	Determines percentage base for category variables
FTOTAL, PTOTAL	Creates stand-in variables for totals within tables
GBASE	Determines percentage base for multiple-response variables
MDGROUP, MRGROUP	Creates multiple-response variables
MISSING	Determines treatment of missing values
OBSERVATION	Declares variables to be summarized rather than counted

Local subcommands (see Table 2) except STATISTICS can be repeated once for each table created. STATISTICS can be repeated within each table. TABLE must come first. Local subcommands apply only to the preceding TABLE subcommand.

Table 2   Local subcommands

Subcommand	Explanation
CAPTION	Creates the caption cell for individual tables
CORNER	Creates labels for the corner area in a table
SORT	Sorts cells of individual tables
STATISTICS	Indicates statistics to be calculated
TABLE	Determines structure of individual tables
TITLE	Creates a title for individual tables

Usage of some subcommands changed as of SPSS 7.0 (see Table 3). Continued use of any of the following subcommands will result in a warning message or failure of the request. In all cases, the subcommand was replaced by a function, as noted.

Table 3   Subcommands that changed as of SPSS 7.0

Subcommand	Explanation
BOXCHARS	Subcommand is ignored, function replaced by metafile rendering.
CONTINUED	Subcommand is ignored, function replaced by Page Setup on the File menu of the Viewer.
FOOTNOTE	Subcommand is aliased to CAPTION.
FORMAT	With the exception of BLANK/ZERO and the MISSING keyword, the FORMAT subcommand is ignored. Function replaced by TableLook and Table Properties on the Format menu in the Pivot Table Editor.
INDEX	Subcommand is ignored, function replaced by the outline side of the Viewer.
)PAGE	When keyword is used within titles and captions it is ignored with a warning. Function replaced by Page Setup on the File menu of the Viewer.
PFOOTNOTE	Subcommand is ignored, function replaced by Page Setup on the File Menu of the Viewer.
PTITLE	Subcommand is ignored, function replaced by Page Setup on the File menu of the Viewer.
TFOOTNOTE	Subcommand is aliased to CAPTION. The CENTER, LEFT, and RIGHT options are eliminated with a warning. Function replaced by Table Properties on the Format menu in the Pivot Table Editor.
TTITLE	Subcommand is aliased to TITLE. The CENTER, LEFT, and RIGHT options are eliminated with a warning. The TITLE subcommand produces the title cell.
WRITE	Subcommand is eliminated.

Variables

Five types of variables and "stand-in" variables are available in the Tables procedure, as listed below. Category variables are the default. The rest are declared or created with global subcommands.

Category   *Classification of data.* Any variable that is in the active file and not named on an OBSERVATION subcommand is treated as a category variable whose values classify the data.

Observation   *Variables for summary statistics.* The OBSERVATION subcommand identifies variables in the active file whose values are used to compute summary statistics.

Multiple response   *Summary variables for multiple-response items.* The MDGROUP and MRGROUP subcommands create multiple-response variables from elementary variables in the active file. When MDGROUP is used to create the multiple-response variable, it tallies occurrences of a specified value in each of the elementary variables. When MRGROUP is used to create the multiple-response variable, it tallies occurrences of each distinct value in all the elementary variables.

Following total   *Totals that follow the items they summarize.* The FTOTAL subcommand creates a total, a variable-like syntax device that reserves a row, column, or layer for summary statistics. The statistics are for the item that the total follows on the TABLE subcommand, and they appear following that item in the table that is produced.

Preceding total   *Totals that precede the items they summarize.* Like FTOTAL, the PTOTAL subcommand creates a total. However, the associated summary statistics are for the item that the total precedes on the TABLE subcommand, and they appear preceding that item in the table that is produced.

Relations among Variables

Variables (and totals) on a TABLE subcommand can be combined in several ways to specify the design of a table. All the types of variables can enter into such combinations, but some restrictions apply (see the section on the TABLE subcommand). The relations that can combine variables are:

BY   *Dimensions.* The keyword BY separates the variables or combinations of variables that are assigned to different table dimensions. The first BY on a TABLE subcommand separates the row expression from the column expression, and the second BY separates the column expression from the layer expression.

+   *Stacking.* A variable that is stacked with another variable is added next to it along the same dimension, in effect creating a new table that is an extension of the original.

>   *Nesting.* When a variable is nested within another (the controlling variable), the resulting table displays all values of the nested variable after each value of the controlling variable. The control variable is specified before the nesting operator, and the nested variable, after.

( )   *Changed order of joining with nesting.* In an expression containing both joining and nesting, the default order of operations is nesting first. Parentheses can change the order in either of two ways. The expression SEX > (STORE + REGION) specifies that the joining of *store* and *region* will be nested within *sex*. The expression (SEX + STORE) > REGION is a shorthand expression that is expanded into SEX > REGION joined with STORE > REGION.

Statistics

Four subcommands affect the statistics that appear in the tables. The first three listed below are global, and the last is local.

BASE   *Percentage base.* Defines missing-value handling for the variables that define the base used in calculating percentages.

GBASE   *Multiple-response variable percentage base.* Determines the type of count (cases or responses) for the percentage base used with multiple-response variables.

MISSING   *Missing values.* Determines the treatment of cases with user-missing values for variables named on the VARIABLES subcommand.

STATISTICS   *Cell statistics.* Specifies the functions used to compute counts, percentages, and other statistics that form the content of table cells. This subcommand also determines the display dimension, controlling whether the functions create rows, columns, or layers.

TableLook Setting

The TLOOK subcommand on the SET command instructs the TABLES command to use a specific TableLook, which is a set of properties that defines the appearance of a table. Each TableLook consists of a collection of table properties, including general appearance, footnote properties, cell properties, and borders. The default is NONE, which uses the TableLook provided as the system default. You can define a TableLook in the Pivot Table Editor.

Table Layout

The layout of a table is predetermined by the specified or default TableLook. Once the table is created, it can be customized by using the Pivot Table Editor. Three subcommands on the TABLES command affect table layout. The first two subcommands listed below are global, and the last one is local.

AUTOLABEL   *Level of automatic labeling.* Instructs the TABLES command to use the level of automatic labeling and titling that you want, which can include variable names when no labels exist, values when no value labels are found, statistical function names when no labels are provided, a default header and the page number as the page title, and the TABLE subcommand as the default table title.

FORMAT   *Printing characteristics.* Dictates the appearance of data within a table by specifying BLANK|ZERO or MISSING characters. Complete format defaults are available through the default TableLook on the Pivot Table Editor.

CORNER   *Corner label*. Lines of text in the box that is above the row titles and next to the column titles. Note that to view text in the CORNER you must set the row dimension labels as nested in Table Properties on the Format menu in the Pivot Table Editor.

Table Size

The size of a table depends on the number of row, column and layer categories specified. The output generated may be reorganized in the Pivot Table Editor prior to printing. Tables may be scaled to fit the page when printed in Table Properties on the Format menu in the Pivot Table Editor. The number of printed pages depends on the size of the table.

Length

In addition to the default TableLook, the length of a table varies according to:

- The number of row variables and the number of values for each (see the TABLE subcommand).
- The number of statistics requested for row variables (see the STATISTICS subcommand).
- The number of lines for labels, including the number of additional lines for labels that wrapped because they exceeded the column width (see "Labels" on p. 156).
- The number of lines for titles and footnotes (see the TITLE and FOOTNOTE subcommands).

The length of a table can be reduced by:

- Null variable and value labels that remove lines allotted for explicit labels.
- A null statistic label in the rows for the first function requested.
- Null labels for all the statistics in a dimension.
- Smaller fonts and margins in the TableLook.

Width

In addition to the default TableLook the width of a table varies according to:

- The number of column variables and the number of values for each (see the TABLE subcommand).
- The number of statistics requested for column variables (see the STATISTICS subcommand).

The width of a table can be reduced by:

- Specifying the row dimension for statistics so they are stacked in the cells (see the STATISTICS subcommand).
- Smaller fonts and margins in the TableLook.

Layers

The number of layers depends on:

- The number of layer variables and the number of values for each (see the TABLE subcommand).
- The number of statistics requested across the layers (see the STATISTICS subcommand).

The number of layers can be reduced by moving layer variables to the rows or columns as control variables for nestings.

Pages

The number of pages that is generated depends on:
- The number of TABLE subcommands.
- The number of layers in each table.
- Paper size and margins are specified in the Page Setup dialog box.

Labels

The Tables procedure uses labels defined by the VARIABLE LABELS and VALUE LABELS commands. The Tables procedure also lets you create variable labels for group variables specified on the MDGROUP and MRGROUP subcommands, labels for totals specified on the FTOTAL and PTOTAL subcommands, and labels for statistics whose functions are named on the STATISTICS subcommand. See the individual sections on these subcommands for the complete syntax to use in specifying the labels. The settings on the Output Labels tab of the Options dialog box determine whether the Variable Labels or Value Labels will display in the Viewer.

The syntax for defining labels on a VARIABLE LABELS command or on a VALUE LABELS command is:

```
VARIABLE LABELS varname 'label' [/varname...]
VALUE LABELS varlist value 'label' value 'label'...[/varlist...]
```

The following general rules apply to labels on the TABLES command:

- A variable label can be up to 120 characters long. (When MDGROUP uses elementary variable labels as value labels for a group variable, it retains up to 120 characters for each label.)
- A statistic label can be up to 120 characters long.
- When string values are used instead of labels, they are truncated to short strings.
- A value label can be up to 60 characters long.
- A label that is longer than the established column width is wrapped onto one or more additional lines until the entire label is printed.

- A value label assigned to a value that does not exist never appears in a table.
- Title, footnote, caption, and corner text lines are not labels. Each can be up to 10 lines of text. Corner text not fitting inside the corner will not increase the size of the corner area.

Example

```
VARIABLE LABELS VAR1
    'This is an example of a variable label that is ' +
    'very long.  It shows how the long ' +
    'label appears in the rows.'.
VALUE LABELS VAR1
    1 'This is how Tables handles a value label with 60 characters.'
    2 'Another example of a long value label in the procedure.'
    3 'This value does not exist.'.
TABLES FORMAT =
        /TABLE = VAR1+VAR2 BY VAR3.
```

| | | VAR3 | |
		1.00	2.00
This is an example of a variable label that is very long. It shows how the long label appears in the rows.	This is how Tables handles a value label with 60 characters.	2	2
	Another example of a long value label in the procedure.	2	2
VAR2	1.00	2	2
	2.00	2	2

- Variable *var1* has long variable and value labels. Since the length exceeds the width of the row title column, the labels occupy multiple lines.
- The value label for value 3 of variable *var1* does not appear in the table, since that value does not exist in the data.
- Variables *var2* and *var3* have no variable labels, so the variable names are printed.
- Variables *var2* and *var3* have no value labels, so the values are printed.

Blank and Null Labels

Blank labels and null labels are different from each other and have different effects:
- A blank label for a variable, value, or statistic (' ') is treated as a valid label, and the Tables procedure provides a blank line where a text label would normally print.
- A null variable or value label ('') removes the line allotted for the label.

- A null statistic label (' ') for the first function specified for the stub causes the cell contents to rise one line, thus beginning on the same line as the value label.
- A null statistic label (' ') for a function after the first specified for the stub produces no label but leaves a blank line.

Example

```
VARIABLE LABELS VAR1 ' 'VAR3' '.
VALUE LABELS VAR2 1 ' '/VAR4 1 ' '.
TABLES
        /TABLE = VAR1 + VAR2 BY VAR3 + VAR4 + VAR5 + VAR6
        /STATISTICS = CPCT(VAR3) CPCT(VAR4' ') CPCT(VAR5'%').
```

				VAR4		VAR5		VAR6	
		1.00	2.00			1.00	2.00		
		Count Percent	Count Percent		2.00	%	%	1.00	2.00
	1.00	25.0%	25.0%	25.0%	25.0%	25.0%	25.0%	2	2
	2.00	25.0%	25.0%	25.0%	25.0%	25.0%	25.0%	2	2
VAR2		25.0%	25.0%	25.0%	25.0%	25.0%	25.0%	2	2
	2.00	25.0%	25.0%	25.0%	25.0%	25.0%	25.0%	2	2

- The variable *var1* has a blank label, and *var3* has a null label. The row title for *var1* shows a blank line, while the column title for *var3* doesn't show any space for the variable name.
- The value 1 has a null label for *var2* and a blank label for *var4*. This moves the row title for *var2* down into the row for value 1 of that variable and leaves a blank space for value 1 of *var4*.
- Statistics (percentages) are explicitly assigned to *var3*, *var4*, and *var5*. The variable *var3* has the default label, *var4* has a null label, and *var5* has a specified label.
- The variable *var6* gets the default statistic (count) with no label, because no statistics were requested.

Wrapping Labels

The following general rules for the TABLES command apply to label wrapping:

- Labels wrap to the next line by default when they are too long for the column width.
- The table formats uses blanks as the points for wrapping. It removes the blank where a label is wrapped and adjusts the continuation of the label appropriately within the column.
- A word, defined by surrounding blanks, is broken when the entire word does not fit within the column width.

Errors

A syntax error of any kind in the Tables procedure prevents the procedure from executing. Syntax errors include title, footnote, caption, and corner text lines that are too wide for the space allotted by the TableLook. When an error is detected, the procedure continues to check for other errors but does not read the data.

General Limitations

The upper limits set for various aspects of the Tables procedure are:

- 100 observation variables.
- 100 category variables.
- 100 elementary variables on all group variable subcommands.
- 20 group variables for MDGROUP and MRGROUP.
- 20 totals for FTOTAL.
- 20 totals for PTOTAL.
- 10 separate text lines for each multiple-line title in the TITLE, FOOTNOTE, and CORNER subcommands.
- 120 characters for variable labels, statistics labels, and MDGROUP value labels.
- 60 characters for value labels.
- 255 characters for each title line.

AUTOLABEL

```
/AUTOLABEL {DEFAULT}
          {ON     }
          {OFF    }
```

Overview

AUTOLABEL is a global subcommand. It instructs the Tables procedure to use one of the following levels of labeling:

DEFAULT   *Variable names, variable values, and function names.* Prints a variable name when no variable label is found, a value when no value label is found, and a statistical function name when a function is explicitly requested but no label is provided.

ON   *Title defaults and other defaults.* Supplies the automatic labels provided with the DEFAULT keyword, a default table title consisting of the TABLE subcommand, and a default page title.

OFF   *No defaults.* Turns off all default labeling and uses only the titles and the variable, value, and statistics labels that are explicitly given.

Operations

- When testing several different table designs, use AUTOLABEL=ON to provide table titles that clearly identify the alternatives.
- Use OFF when running tables that have unusual values or obvious variable names that are not required, such as *sex* when you have the explicit value labels *Male* and *Female*.

BASE

```
/BASE = {ANSWERING}
        {QUALIFIED}
        {ALL      }
```

Example:

```
TABLES MISSING = INCLUDE
       /BASE = QUALIFIED
       /TABLE = USINTL BY SEX
       /STATISTICS = CPCT (USINTL:SEX).
```

			Respondent's Sex	
			Male	Female
Take Active Part in World Affairs	NAP	Count Percent	33.5%	31.8%
	Active Part	Count Percent	52.5%	47.4%
	Stay Out	Count Percent	13.1%	18.6%
	DK	Count Percent	.9%	2.2%

Overview

BASE is a global subcommand. It determines how missing values are handled for the variables that define a percentage base.

ANSWERING *Excludes missing values.* This is the default. When a percentage base is calculated, this option excludes cases with missing values.

QUALIFIED *Includes user-missing values.* When a percentage base is calculated, this option includes cases with user-missing values.

ALL *Includes all missing values.* When a percentage base is calculated, this option includes cases with system- and user-missing values.

Operations

- The handling of missing values for the percentage base should normally correspond to the specification on the MISSING subcommand. However, use BASE=ALL when you want the percentage base to include all the cases regardless of the MISSING specification.
- If you have more than one BASE subcommand, only the last one is in effect.
- To clean the appearance of the table, the redundant labels (*Respondent's Sex* and *Count Percent*) could be deleted in the Pivot Table Editor.

161

BREAK

```
/BREAK BY expression
```

Overview

BREAK is a global subcommand. It allows you to specify an expression that is appended to every TABLE subcommand in the TABLES command, thereby repeating the expression without reentering it.

Operations

- The argument to BREAK BY can be any expression that yields valid syntax when appended to every TABLE subcommand in the TABLES command.
- You can break the TABLE subcommand at any symbol, except in the middle of a variable name.

Example:

In the following TABLES command, each TABLE subcommand ends with the same expression.

```
TABLES
/ TABLE =  (a+b)    BY d>(e+f)
/ TABLE =        c  BY d>(e+f)
/ TABLE =  (a+b)>c  BY d>(e+f)
/ TABLE =  (a+b)>c  BY d>(e+f)
/ TABLE =   a+b+c   BY d>(e+f).
```

Using BREAK, the command can be stated as:

```
TABLES/ BREAK BY d>(e+f)
/ TABLE =  (a+b)
/ TABLE =        c
/ TABLE =  (a+b)>c
/ TABLE =  (a+b)>c
/ TABLE =   a+b+c.
```

CAPTION and TITLE

```
/{TITLE   } = [.........]
 {CAPTION } [..........]
```

Overview

TITLE and CAPTION are local subcommands. They provide lines of text for a title and a caption for the table specified on the preceding TABLE subcommand.

Operations

- If AUTOLABEL=ON, the default for TITLE is the TABLE subcommand. If AUTOLABEL= DEFAULT or OFF, no default table title is supplied.
- Table title lines print at the top of the table.
- Table caption lines print at the bottom of the table and before any footnotes.
- If multiple TITLE or CAPTION subcommands follow the same TABLE subcommand, only the last one is in effect.

Limitations

- Caption and title subcommands accept no more than 10 lines of text.

Functions

Both TITLE and CAPTION recognize the)DATE function for use in the lines of text.)DATE must be entered in upper case.

- The)DATE function prints numbers for the day, month, and year separated by spaces.

Example

```
SORT CASES BY SEX.
SPLIT FILE BY SEX.
TABLES
        /TABLE = USINTL BY RACE
        /TITLE =     ')DATE' '' '' 'Title'
```

12 Oct 95

Title

				Race of Respondent		
				White	Black	Other
Respondent's Sex	Male	Take Active Part in World Affairs	Active Part	295	29	10
			Stay Out	70	11	2
	Female	Take Active Part in World Affairs	Active Part	359	49	10
			Stay Out	124	36	4

CORNER

```
/CORNER = ['line' 'line'...]
```

Overview

CORNER is a local subcommand. It places lines of text in the box that is above the row titles and next to the column titles. You can specify multiple lines of text, but each must fit within the row title column width. There is no default text for the corner box.

Operations

- If you specify more lines than are available in the corner, the TABLES command prints as many lines as will fit. Use the Cell Properties Alignment tab on the Format menu in the Pivot Table Editor to set the alignment of the text.
- If the default TableLook uses the Corner format, which reserves the corner for dimension labels in the rows, text specified in syntax will not appear in the Output Navigator. To view text in the corner you must have the Row Dimension Labels set as Nested in Table Properties on the Format menu in the Pivot Table Editor. Note this option may be preset in the default TableLook.

Limitations

- The CORNER subcommand accepts no more than 10 lines of text.

FORMAT

```
/FORMAT = [{BLANK}]        [MISSING ({'.'     })]
          {ZERO }                   {'chars'}
```

Overview

FORMAT is a global subcommand. It controls the appearance of data within tables by specifying BLANK, ZERO or MISSING characters. Complete format settings are available through TableLook and Table Properties in the Pivot Table Editor.

Operations

These options define characters for empty cells and for missing data in cells.

MISSING('chars')   *Characters for missing data.* Defines special fill characters for cells with missing data. For example, if the data for a category variable are missing in a cell, the MISSING characters become the cell contents (see the STATISTICS subcommand).

- The default for MISSING characters is a single period.
- MISSING(' ') leaves the cell contents blank.
- Up to 255 characters can be specified.
- The specified character string is right-justified in the spaces for the statistical format.
- If there are more MISSING characters than there are spaces for the statistical format, the character string is allowed to extend into any available column spaces to the left of the format. If the additional spaces are still not enough, the character string is truncated from the right.

BLANK   *Blank empty cells.* Leaves empty cells blank.

ZERO   *Zeros in empty cells.* Prints zeros in empty cells according to the statistical format. For example, with an F4.1 format, a zero value prints as .0 in the cell.

FTOTAL and PTOTAL

```
/FTOTAL = varname ['label'] varname ...
/PTOTAL = varname ['label'] varname ...
```

Example:

```
TABLES
        /FTOTAL = FTOT
        /PTOTAL = PTOT
        /TABLE = USINTL + FTOT BY PTOT + REGION.
```

		PTOT	Region of the United States		
			North East	South East	West
Take Active Part in World Affairs	Active Part	**752**	327	207	218
	Stay Out	**247**	112	68	67
FTOT		**999**	**439**	**275**	**285**

- FTOTAL or PTOTAL is followed by a list of variable names, each of which is optionally followed by a variable label in apostrophes or quotation marks.

- No reserved keywords can be used as the variable names.

- The variable names cannot conflict with category, observation, or multiple-response variable names on the same TABLES command. They can, however, duplicate other variable names in the working data file.

- More than one FTOTAL or PTOTAL subcommand can be specified before the first TABLE subcommand.

Overview

Both FTOTAL and PTOTAL are global subcommands. They produce summary statistics by using **totals**, syntax devices that function like temporary variables. Totals hold summary statistics for the items they either follow or precede on a TABLE subcommand. Totals that follow the items they summarize are declared on FTOTAL, and totals that precede their summarized items are declared on PTOTAL. The position of the summary statistics in the table that is produced corresponds to the type of total. The statistics for following totals are displayed in the column, row, or layer following the summarized items, and the statistics for preceding totals precede the summarized items. The function of totals in the table structure is discussed with the TABLE subcommand. The statistics available for totals are discussed with the STATISTICS subcommand.

Operations

- If no optional label is specified for a total, the variable name for the total is used as the label.
- The same variable name for a total can be used more than once on a TABLE subcommand, because the total serves as a place holder. However, using the same name more than once may result in failure of the total to pick up the correct statistic and may result in an error when statistics are explicitly applied to variables in the table.

Limitations

- A total variable name can be no more than 8 characters long, and its label can be no more than 120 characters long.
- You can declare no more than 20 following totals and 20 preceding totals.

GBASE

```
/GBASE = {CASES    }
         {RESPONSES}
```

Overview

GBASE is a global subcommand. It specifies the count used for the percentage base with multiple-response variables.

CASES   *Cases as the denominator.* Bases percentages on the number of respondents (cases). This option is the default.

RESPONSES   *Responses as the denominator.* Bases percentages on the number of responses.

The GBASE subcommand does not alter the missing-value treatment specified on the MISSING and BASE subcommands. It is used in addition to those subcommands to determine the desired count for the denominator when percentages are requested for multiple-response variables. (See "STATISTICS: Percentage Bases" on p. 192.)

Operations

- Conventionally, percentages are calculated with the same type of count for both the numerator and the denominator—either cases or responses for both.
- You can request cases for the numerator and responses for the denominator by specifying COUNT or CASES on the STATISTICS subcommand and RESPONSES on the GBASE subcommand.
- You can request responses for the numerator and cases for the denominator by specifying RESPONSES on the STATISTICS subcommand and by leaving cases (the default) for GBASE.

MDGROUP and MRGROUP

```
/MDGROUP = varname ['label'] varlist ({value  })
                                      {'chars'}
/MRGROUP = varname ['label'] varlist
```

Example:

```
TABLES
      /MDGROUP = MDVAR 'Health and Work Problems (dichotomy vars)'
        HLTH1 TO WORK9 (1)
      /MRGROUP = MRVAR 'Problems (multi-category vars)'
        PROB1 TO PROB4
      /TABLE = MRVAR + MDVAR BY SEX.
```

		Respondent's Sex	
		Male	Female
Problems (multi-category vars)	Health	48	90
	Finances	83	125
	Lack of Basic Services	4	3
	Family	23	53
	Personal	15	26
	Legal	1	1
	Miscellaneous	23	48
Health and Work Problems (dichotomy vars)	Ill Enough to Go to a Doctor	185	374
	Counselling for Mental Problems	18	40
	Infertility, Unable to Have a Baby	9	26
	Drinking Problem	9	8
	Illegal Drugs (Marijuana, Cocaine)	23	7
	Partner (Husband, Wife) In Hospital	37	36
	Child in Hospital	25	53
	Child on Drugs, Drinking Problem	6	22
	Death of a Close Friend	99	131
	Unemployed and Looking for Work a Month +	36	23
	Being Demoted or Move to Worse Position	10	16
	Cut in Pay or Reduced Hours	36	25
	Being Passed Over for Promotion	18	20
	Having Trouble with One's Boss	21	21
	Own Business Losing Money or Failing	11	9
	Partner (Husband, Wife) Being Fired	8	17
	Partner (Husband, Wife) Cut in Pay	18	34
	One's Spouse Being Unemployed	24	31

- The variable name following the subcommand name identifies a multiple-response set. The variable list after the multiple-response set specifies elementary variables.
- Elementary variables can be numeric or short string. The type of the first elementary variable determines the type of its multiple-response set.
- Multiple-response sets function like category variables and can be nested or joined with any type of variable.

Overview

MDGROUP and MRGROUP are global subcommands. They are usually used for tabulating multiple-response questions, each of which allows more than one answer from a respondent. Each subcommand creates a multiple-response set that combines elementary variables.

MDGROUP combines elementary variables that are dichotomous. Typically, each dichotomous elementary variable records the presence of a different response. Any elementary variables with a particular coded value show the presence of a response. All other values show the absence of the response. For all of the elementary variables, the coded value is the same, and this value must be specified on the MDGROUP subcommand. The multiple-response set holds a count of the value's occurrences for each elementary variable.

The typical use of the MRGROUP subcommand is to combine elementary variables that contain a different value for each of the possible responses. Summing across all cases and all elementary variables, the multiple-response set holds counts for each occurrence of a different value in the elementary variables.

Operations

- An error results if you mix numeric and string elementary variables for one multiple-response set.
- If you do not specify a label for a multiple-response variable, its name is used instead.
- Each MDGROUP or MRGROUP subcommand creates only one multiple-response set. Multiple subcommands must be used to create several such variables when you tabulate more than one multiple-response question.

MDGROUP Subcommand

- The value to be tallied by MDGROUP must be specified. There is no default.
- The specified value should match the type of the elementary variables, numeric or string.
- An MDGROUP elementary variable can have more than two values. The variable is still effectively dichotomous, because only the specified value is used and the others are ignored.
- The names or labels of the elementary variables become the value labels for the multiple-response variable.

MRGROUP Subcommand

- MRGROUP variables have no limit on the number of distinct values allowed. A value or value label for the multiple-response variable is displayed for every distinct value found in the elementary variables.
- The value labels for the multiple-response variable are taken from the first elementary variables that have labels for the individual values.
- If a value label is not available, the Tables procedure uses the value itself as a label and displays it using the print format from the first elementary variable. If the print formats differ across variables, name the elementary variable with the desired print format first.

Limitations

- A multiple-response variable name can be no more than 8 characters long, and its label can be no more than 120 characters long.
- No more than 20 multiple-response variables can be created with any combination of MDGROUP and MRGROUP subcommands.
- All MDGROUP or MRGROUP subcommands on a table can combine up to 100 elementary variables into multiple-response variables.

MISSING

```
/MISSING = {EXCLUDE}
          {INCLUDE}
```

Overview

MISSING is a global subcommand. It determines the treatment of cases with user-missing values. System-missing values are never considered valid.

EXCLUDE   *User-missing values are invalid.* This is the default.

INCLUDE   *User-missing values are valid.*

INCLUDE on the MISSING subcommand should ordinarily correspond to QUALIFIED on the BASE subcommand, and EXCLUDE should correspond to ANSWERING. For example, it is typical that when MISSING=INCLUDE, BASE=QUALIFIED.

Operations

- User-missing values that are included in a table are treated like any other values.
- If you have more than one MISSING subcommand, the last one overrides the others preceding it.

The effect of MISSING=EXCLUDE differs according to the types of variables and statistical functions that are requested:

- If a case has a missing value for a category variable, the case is excluded from a table using that variable.
- If a case has a missing value for an elementary variable of a multiple-response variable, the elementary variable is excluded from the multiple-response variable. The case itself is not excluded, however, because it may have valid values for other elementary variables.
- If a case has a missing value for an observation variable, the case is excluded from summary statistics (such as the mean, sum, and standard deviation) for that variable. The case is also excluded from the VALIDN and VPCT functions.
- If a case has a missing value for an observation variable, the case is not excluded from COUNT or CPCT. These functions are affected only by missing values for category or group variables.

MRGROUP

See "MDGROUP and MRGROUP" on p. 170.

OBSERVATION

```
/OBSERVATION = varlist
```

Example:

```
TABLES /OBSERVATION = AGE EDUC
       /TABLE = (AGE + EDUC) > REGION BY SEX.
```

			Respondent's Sex	
			Male	Female
Age of Respondent	Region of the United States	North East	44	47
		South East	46	49
		West	43	44
Highest Year of School Completed	Region of the United States	North East	13	13
		South East	13	12
		West	13	13

- Observation variables must be numeric.
- More than one OBSERVATION subcommand can be used before the first TABLE subcommand to add observation variables to the list.

Overview

OBSERVATION is a global subcommand. It identifies variables in the working data file whose values are used to compute summary statistics such as the sum, mean, and standard deviation. The function of observation variables in the table structure is discussed with the TABLE subcommand. The statistics available for observation variables are discussed with the STATISTICS subcommand.

Operations

- Specified variable labels are used as labels for observation variables. If no variable labels are specified, variable names are used instead.
- An observation variable can be used as an elementary variable for an MDGROUP or MRGROUP subcommand.
- To clean the appearance of the table, the redundant labels (*Respondent's Sex* and *Region of the United States*) could be deleted in the Pivot Table Editor.

Limitations

- The Tables procedure allows a maximum of 100 observation variables.

PTOTAL

See "FTOTAL and PTOTAL" on p. 167.

SORT

```
/SORT [{DESCENDING}] VAR1[(FUNCTION1[OBS1])] [VAR2 ...]
      {ASCENDING }
```

Example:

```
TABLES
  /FTOTAL = TOTAL
  /OBSERVATION = AGE
  /TABLE = HAPPY BY AGE + REGION + TOTAL
  /SORT = HAPPY
  /TABLE = HAPPY BY AGE + REGION + TOTAL
  /SORT = HAPPY(MEAN(AGE)).
```

| | | Age of Respondent | Region of the United States | | | TOTAL |
			North East	South East	West	
General Happiness	Pretty Happy	45	412	215	245	**872**
	Very Happy	47	185	149	133	**467**
	Not Too Happy	46	76	47	42	**165**

.

| | | Age of Respondent | Region of the United States | | | TOTAL |
			North East	South East	West	
General Happiness	Very Happy	47	185	149	133	**467**
	Not Too Happy	46	76	47	42	**165**
	Pretty Happy	45	412	215	245	**872**

- In the first table, the cells of *happy* are sorted so that the row with the largest total comes first. The observation variable does not affect the sort.
- In the second table, the cells of *happy* are sorted so that the row with the largest mean comes first. The values in the columns produced by *region* do not affect the sort.

Overview

SORT is a local subcommand. It sorts the cells of a table by their contents.

DESCENDING   *Sorts in descending order.* Sorts the cells of the requested variables so that the row, column, or layer with the highest total comes first. This is the default.

ASCENDING   *Sorts in ascending order.* Sorts the cells of the requested variables so that the row, column, or layer with the lowest total comes first.

- At least one variable must be specified on the SORT subcommand. Additional variables are optional.
- Only category and MRGROUP variables may be SORT variables.
- A function may be specified along with the variable to identify the cells controlling the sort. If no function is mentioned, the variable's COUNT marginals are used.
- Functions explicitly specified for the sort must be defined for the table. That is, those functions must be shown somewhere in the table.
- PTILE, MODE, or MEDIAN may not be sort functions.
- A function may be accompanied by a variable in parentheses. The variable specified must use the base statistic somewhere in the table.

Operations

When you specify multiple variables on the SORT subcommand, the order in which variables are sorted is determined by their order in a table dimension. If they are nested, variables listed first will have their cells sorted before later variables. Variables in different dimensions control only the dimension in which they appear.

When the cells of a sorted variable contain different statistics, the sort function will be determined according to the following rules:

- If you explicitly specify a function (and a variable), that function controls the sort.
- If there is no explicit function, the sort will be on the marginals (totals on the variable sorted).

STATISTICS

```
/STATISTICS = [{UNWEIGHTED}]
               {U          }

    function[([varname] [(fmt)] ['label'] varname...)] function...
```

Functions for all variable types:

COUNT
CPCT

Functions for totals and observation variables:

APTILE	MEDIAN	RPTILE	VALIDN
EPTILE	MINIMUM	SEMEAN	VARIANCE
HPTILE	MODE	SPCT	VPCT
MAXIMUM	PTILE value	STDDEV	WPTILE
MEAN	RANGE	SUM	

Functions for group variables and their totals:

CASES
CSPCT
RESPONSES
RPCT

Formats:

COMMAw.d	NEQUALw.d
DOLLARw.d	PARENw.d
DOTw.d	PCTw.d
Fw.d	PCTPARENw.d
NEGPARENw.d	CCAw.d—CCEw.d

Example:

```
TABLES
    /TABLE = USINTL BY SEX
    /STATISTICS = CPCT (USINTL (PCT7) '').
```

		Respondent's Sex	
		Male	Female
Take Active Part in World Affairs	Active Part	33%	42%
	Stay Out	8%	16%

- Variables named on the STATISTICS subcommand must also be named on the preceding TABLE subcommand and the variables must both be in the same dimension.
- All of the optional items following a function on the STATISTICS subcommand must be enclosed in a set of parentheses.
- If specified, a variable name must precede its format and label, which apply only to that variable.
- More than one variable and label can be named for a single function.
- Functions can be repeated.

Overview

STATISTICS is a local subcommand, applying only to the preceding TABLE subcommand. The STATISTICS subcommand determines the functions used to compute statistics. It also determines whether the statistics labels are above the columns, beside the rows, or above the layers. Functions available to STATISTICS include counts, percentages, and means. The STATISTICS subcommand is optional. When it is not present, default statistics are applied.

For information on bases for percentage statistics, see "STATISTICS: Percentage Bases" on p. 192. For information on the treatment of missing values in the calculation of statistics, see the MISSING subcommand.

Operations

- The position of statistics labels (above the columns, beside the rows, or above the layers) is the same as the position of the variable(s) named on the STATISTICS subcommand. All such variables must be in the same dimension.
- Functions can be applied only to category and group variables that are at the lowest level of a nesting, but they can be applied to observation variables at any level of a nesting.

- If a category variable or a group variable is in a nesting relationship with an observation variable, and statistical functions are named for both the nested variable and the control variable, the Tables procedure uses only the functions for the observation variable and ignores the others.

- For category variables, the default function is COUNT; for observation variables, MEAN; and for multiple-response variables, CASES. For totals, the default is the statistical function for the item that is summarized.

- A function uses weighted cases unless the function name is preceded by U or UNWEIGHTED.

- A function label appears on the line below a variable name or label. However, when the function label applies to an observation variable with a category variable nested within it, the function label follows the value label for the category variable. For more information on labels, see "Labels" on p. 156.

Position of Statistics

The default position of statistics labels is determined by the position of variables named on the STATISTICS subcommand. Only one dimension can be used for statistics. The dimension in which statistics are requested is called the **statistics dimension**. When there is no STATISTICS subcommand, statistics are applied to column variables.

- If a variable is in the statistics dimension but is not assigned a function on the STATISTICS subcommand, that variable receives its normal default function with a null function label.

- Any variable assigned a function receives only that function and not the default function.

- If a function is requested but a variable is not specified, that function becomes assigned to all variables in the statistics dimension to which it can be applied. The function is said to be implicitly applied to those variables.

Example

```
TABLES
        /TABLE = REGION BY SEX + RACE
        /STATISTICS = CPCT(SEX)
        /TABLE = REGION BY SEX + RACE
        /STATISTICS = CPCT COUNT(SEX).
```

		Respondent's Sex		Race of Respondent		
		Male	Female			
		Count Percent	Count Percent	White	Black	Other
Region of the United States	North East	18.5%	26.2%	582	82	15
	South East	11.7%	15.7%	307	94	14
	West	11.7%	16.2%	375	28	20

		Respondent's Sex				Race of Respondent		
		Male		Female		White	Black	Other
		Count Percent	Count	Count Percent	Count	Count Percent	Count Percent	Count Percent
Region of the United States	North East	18.5%	281	26.2%	398	38.4%	5.4%	1.0%
	South East	11.7%	177	15.7%	238	20.2%	6.2%	.9%
	West	11.7%	178	16.2%	245	24.7%	1.8%	1.3%

- The statistics dimension in the first table is determined by the variable specified on the STATISTICS subcommand. Since *sex* is specified for CPCT, the statistics dimension is the columns.

- The default statistic for categorical variables is COUNT. Since no statistics are assigned to *race*, counts are shown. Count percentages are explicitly assigned to *sex*. Therefore, count percentages are shown instead of the default.

- The statistics dimension in the second table is also determined by the variable specified on the STATISTICS subcommand. Since *sex* is specified for COUNT, the statistics dimension is the columns.

- In the second table, no variable is specified for CPCT. Count percentages, thus, are implicitly assigned to all variables in the statistics dimension. Since no statistics are explicitly assigned to *race*, only the implicitly assigned statistic (count percentage) is shown. Since counts are explicitly assigned to *sex*, both the implicitly and explicitly assigned statistics are shown for *sex*.

Default Statistics Dimension

When a STATISTICS subcommand does not name a variable, the following rules determine the statistics dimension:

- If there is an observation variable on the TABLE subcommand, and statistics are not explicitly assigned to a variable, then statistics are shown in the dimension with the observation variable.

- If there is no observation variable, the statistics are shown in the columns.

Example

```
TABLES
        /OBSERVATION = AGE
        /TABLE = USINTL BY RACE
        /STATISTICS = COUNT CPCT
        /TABLE = USINTL>AGE BY RACE
        /STATISTICS = MEAN STDDEV.
```

		Race of Respondent					
		White		Black		Other	
		Count	Count Percent	Count	Count Percent	Count	Count Percent
Take Active Part in World Affairs	Active Part	654	65.5%	78	7.8%	20	2.0%
	Stay Out	194	19.4%	47	4.7%	6	.6%

				Race of Respondent		
				White	Black	Other
Take Active Part in World Affairs	Active Part	Age of Respondent	Mean	45	42	41
			Standard Deviation	17	16	15
	Stay Out	Age of Respondent	Mean	50	44	39
			Standard Deviation	21	19	17

- Because the first STATISTICS subcommand does not name a variable and no observation variable is declared, the statistics for the first table appear in the columns.
- The second table contains the observation variable *age* in the rows. The statistics thus appear in the rows, not the columns.

Totals

The default statistics for a total are the functions specified for the cells that are summarized. Because a total's main purpose is to provide these summary statistics, the defaults should generally be used. However, if you need a different statistic for a total, you may need to name the total on the statistical function explicitly.

Example

```
TABLES
      /FTOTAL = FTOT
      /TABLE = SEX BY REGION + FTOT
      /STATISTICS = COUNT(FTOT) CPCT(FTOT)
      /TABLE = SEX BY REGION + FTOT
      /STATISTICS = COUNT(REGION) CPCT(REGION).
```

		Region of the United States			FTOT	
		North East	South East	West	**Count**	**Count Percent**
Respondent's Sex	Male	281	177	178	**636**	**41.9%**
	Female	398	238	245	**881**	**58.1%**

		Region of the United States						FTOT	
		North East		South East		West			
		Count	Count Percent	Count	Count Percent	Count	Count Percent	**Count**	**Count Percent**
Respondent's Sex	Male	281	18.5%	177	11.7%	178	11.7%	**636**	**41.9%**
	Female	398	26.2%	238	15.7%	245	16.2%	**881**	**58.1%**

- When statistics are explicitly assigned to a total, they apply only to the total. In the first table, count and count percentages are assigned to *ftot*. Only the default statistic (COUNT) is shown for *region*.
- The second table shows the same statistics explicitly assigned to *region*. Since *ftot* totals *region*, the default statistic for *ftot* is the same as the statistics explicitly assigned to *region*.

Example

A function requested without a variable becomes an implicit function for any eligible variable (or total) in the statistics dimension. In this way, the default function for a total can be superceded.

```
TABLES
    /FTOTAL = FTOT
    /TABLE = SEX BY REGION + FTOT
    /STATISTICS = COUNT CPCT(REGION)
    /TABLE = SEX BY REGION + FTOT
    /STATISTICS = COUNT(REGION) CPCT.
```

		Region of the United States						FTOT
		North East		South East		West		
		Count	Count Percent	Count	Count Percent	Count	Count Percent	Count
Respondent's Sex	Male	281	18.5%	177	11.7%	178	11.7%	636
	Female	398	26.2%	238	15.7%	245	16.2%	881

		Region of the United States						FTOT
		North East		South East		West		
		Count	Count Percent	Count	Count Percent	Count	Count Percent	Count Percent
Respondent's Sex	Male	281	18.5%	177	11.7%	178	11.7%	41.9%
	Female	398	26.2%	238	15.7%	245	16.2%	58.1%

- In the first table, COUNT is implicitly assigned to all the variables, while CPCT is explicitly assigned to *region*. Thus, counts and count percentages are shown for *region*, while only counts (the implicitly assigned statistic) are shown for the total.

- In the second table, CPCT is implicitly assigned to all the variables, while COUNT is explicitly assigned to *region*. Thus, counts and count percentages are shown for *region*, while only count percentages (the implicitly assigned statistic) are shown for the total.

Example

Like a variable, a total that is explicitly named on the STATISTICS subcommand must be in the statistics dimension. If the total is the only variable explicitly named on the STATISTICS subcommand, the dimension it is in becomes the statistics dimension.

```
TABLES
    /FTOTAL = FTOT1 FTOT2
    /TABLE = SEX + FTOT1 BY REGION + FTOT2
    /STATISTICS = COUNT CPCT(FTOT1).
```

			Region of the United States			
			North East	South East	West	FTOT2
Respondent's Sex	Male	Count	281	177	178	636
	Female	Count	398	238	245	881
FTOT1	Count		679	415	423	1517
	Count Percent		44.8%	27.4%	27.9%	100.0%

- The STATISTICS subcommand specifies CPCT for *ftot1*, thereby changing the statistics dimension to the rows.
- The variable *ftot1* now gets the CPCT and COUNT functions, and *ftot2* summarizes the rows by using the function assigned to each.
- Because the formats assigned to each row are different, the numbers may not line up in the columns. You can specify the number format on the Value tab of the Cell Properties dialog box on the Format menu in the Pivot Table Editor. To activate the Cell Properties, click on the cell you want to format.

Functions

Each statistical function can be applied only to particular types of variables. It receives a default format and label if explicit ones are not given. Functions preceded by the keyword UNWEIGHTED (or U) use unweighted cases, and the word "Unweighted" precedes their function labels.

Functions for All Variable Types

The following functions are available for all the variable types in the Tables procedure:

COUNT   *Number of occurrences of values.* This is the default function for category variables. If requested for group variables or totals of group variables, COUNT produces the same results as CASES. The default label is *Count* when the function is requested explicitly and null when the function is a default. The default format is F5.

CPCT   *Count percentage.* The cell count as a percentage of a specified base (see "STATISTICS: Percentage Bases" on p. 192). For group variables, default percentages are calculated for cases rather than for cell counts, because GBASE=CASES is the default. The default format is PCT5.1, and the default label is *Count (Dimension) %.*

Functions for Totals and Observation Variables

Additional functions are available for numeric observation variables and numeric totals:

MAXIMUM   *Largest value found.* The default format is the variable print format, and the default label is *Maximum.*

MEAN   *Arithmetic mean.* This is the default statistic for an observation variable. The default format is the variable print format. The default label is *Mean* when the function is requested explicitly or implicitly and null when it is the default for an observation variable.

MEDIAN   *The value below which one half of the observations fall.* If the number of observations is even, the mean of the two middle observations is displayed. The default format is the variable print format, and the default label is *Median.*

MINIMUM   *Smallest value found.* The default format is the variable print format, and the default label is *Minimum.*

MODE   *The value that is the most frequent.* If two or more values tie for the most frequent, only the smallest of them is shown. The default format is the variable print format, and the default label is *Mode.*

PTILE value   *Percentile.* The specified value for the percentage may be any number between 0 and 100. The default specification is 50. The default format is the variable print format, and the default label is *Percentile for ###.##,* where *###.##* is the specified value expressed to two decimal places. Five types of percentiles are available via the keywords discussed in "Types of Percentiles" on p. 188.

RANGE   *Difference between the maximum and minimum values.* The default format is the variable print format, and the default label is *Range.*

SEMEAN   *Standard error of the mean.* The default format is the variable print format, and the default label is *Std Err of Mean.*

SPCT   *Sum percentage.* The cell sum as a percentage of a specified base (see "STATISTICS: Percentage Bases" on p. 192). The default format is PCT5.1, and the default label is *(Dimension) Sum %.*

STDDEV   *Standard deviation.* The default format is the variable print format, and the default label is *Std Deviation.*

SUM   *Sum of the values.* The default format is the variable print format, and the default label is *Sum.*

VALIDN   *Count of the nonmissing values of an observation variable.* The default format is F5, and the default label is *Valid N.*

VARIANCE	*Variance of the values.* The default format is the variable print format, and the default label is *Variance*.
VPCT	*Valid count percentage.* The valid cell count as a percentage of a specified base (see "STATISTICS: Percentage Bases" on p. 192). The default format is PCT5.1, and the default label is *Valid N %*.

Types of Percentiles

The following percentiles are available. You can specify as many as you wish, each with a value indicating the percentile you wish to display. In the following formulas, cases are assumed to be ranked in ascending order. The following notation is used: w is the sum of the weights for all nonmissing cases, p is the specified percentile divided by 100, i is the rank of each case, and X_i is the value of the ith case.

HPTILE value	*Weighted average at* $X_{(w+1)p}$. The percentile value is the weighted average of X_i and X_{i+1} using the formula $(1-f)X_i + fX_{i+1}$, where $(w+1)p$ is decomposed into an integer part i and a fractional part f. This is the default calculation for PTILE.
WPTILE value	*Weighted average at* X_{wp}. The percentile value is the weighted average of X_i and $X_{(i+1)}$ using the formula $(1-f)X_i + fX_{i+1}$, where i is the integer part of wp and f is the fractional part of wp.
RPTILE value	*Observation closest to* wp. The percentile value is X_i, where i is the integer part of $(wp + 0.5)$.
EPTILE value	*Empirical distribution function.* The percentile value is X_i when the fractional part of wp is equal to 0. The percentile value is X_{i+1} when the fractional part of wp is greater than 0.
APTILE value	*Empirical distribution with averaging.* The percentile value is $(X_i + X_{i+1})/2$ when the fractional part of wp equals 0. The percentile value is X_{i+1} when the fractional part of wp is greater than 0.

Functions for Group Variables

The following functions are available for group variables and for totals applied to group variables:

CASES	*Count of cases (respondents) for a group variable.* This is the default statistic for group variables. The default format is F5, and the default label is *Cases*.
CSPCT	*Case percentage.* The cell count of cases as a percentage of the specified base. (See "STATISTICS: Percentage Bases" on p. 192. See also the GBASE subcommand.) The default format is PCT5.1, and the default label is *Cases (Dimension) %*.
RESPONSES	*Count of responses for a group variable.* The values shown for each category of the group variable are the same as those shown for CASES. A total of re-

sponses, however, shows responses, not cases. The default format is F5, and the default label is *Responses.*

RPCT   *Response percentage.* The cell count of responses as a percentage of the specified base. (See "STATISTICS: Percentage Bases" on p. 192. See also the GBASE subcommand.) The values shown for each category of the group variable are the same as those shown for CSPCT. A total of response percentages shows responses, not cases. The default format is PCT5.1, and the default label is *Responses (Dimension) %.*

Formats

In all of the formats below, *w* is the overall width and *d* is the number of digits after the decimal point. In all cases, the specification *w* is the same as the specification *w.0*. The following formats are available for use with functions on the STATISTICS subcommand:

COMMAw.d   *Commas between sets of digits.* Width *w* includes a comma before every three digits, a decimal point, and *d* decimal places. For example, 8,210.50 results from a COMMA8.2 format.

DOLLARw.d   *Dollar sign, commas, and decimal point.* Width *w* includes a preceding dollar sign, a comma before every three digits, a decimal point, and *d* decimal places. For example, $8,210.50 results from a DOLLAR9.2 format.

Fw.d   *Standard numeric.* Width *w* includes the decimal point and *d* decimal places. For example, 8210.50 results from an F7.2 format.

NEGPARENw.d   *Parentheses around negative numbers.* Width *w* includes parentheses around a number when it is negative, appropriate commas, a decimal point, and *d* decimal places. For example, (8,210.50) results from a NEGPAREN10.2 format.

NEQUALw.d   N= *preceding the number.* Width *w* includes *N*= preceding the number, a decimal point, and *d* decimal places. For example, *N*=8210.50 results from an NEQUAL9.2 format.

PARENw.d   *Parentheses around the number.* Width *w* includes parentheses, a decimal point, and *d* decimal places. For example, (8210.50) results from a PAREN9.2 format.

PCTw.d   *Percentage.* Width *w* includes a trailing percent sign, a decimal point, and *d* decimal places. For example, 10.50% results from a PCT6.2 format.

PCTPARENw.d   *Parentheses around percentages.* Width *w* includes parentheses around the number, a decimal point, *d* decimal places, and a percent sign. For example, (10.50%) results from a PCTPAREN8.2 format.

• A format that specifies only a *w* value for the width but no *d* for decimal places produces integer results (the default *d* value is 0). For example, 100% results from a PCT4 format.

• If a format width is smaller than a number, but there is a space to the left of the format within the column width, the Tables procedure uses that space to print the number anyway. This rule applies to both default and explicit formats.

- If a column width is too narrow for a number, the Tables procedure first removes dollar signs, commas, parentheses, and percent signs. If the column width is still too narrow, decimal places are dropped until only the integer portion of the number is left. Next, the Tables procedure tries exponential notation. Finally, if exponential notation doesn't fit, the Tables procedure prints asterisks in the cells.

Defaults

- Defaults may be preset in the default TableLook on the Format menu of the Pivot Table Editor.
- For some functions, the default format used for cell contents is the print format of the variable. Other functions have their own specific defaults.
- The default format for a total is ordinarily the format of the function of the item that is summarized. However, a different format can be assigned to a total by using the STATISTICS subcommand.

The following table summarizes the default formats as well as the default labels for statistical functions.

Table 1   Default formats and labels

Function	Default format	Default label
CASES	F5.0	Cases
COUNT	F5.0	Count
CPCT	PCT5.1	Count (Dimension) %
CSPCT	PCT5.1	Cases (Dimension) %
MAXIMUM	variable print format	Maximum
MEAN	variable print format	Mean
MEDIAN	variable print format	Median
MINIMUM	variable print format	Minimum
MODE	variable print format	Mode
PTILE value	variable print format	Percentile for ###.##
RANGE	variable print format	Range
RESPONSES	F5.0	Responses
RPCT	PCT5.1	Responses (Dimension)%
SEMEAN	variable print format	Std Err of Mean
SPCT	PCT5.1	Sum (Dimension) %
STDEV	variable print format	Std Deviation
SUM	variable print format	Sum
VALIDN	F5.0	Valid N
VARIANCE	variable print format	Variance
VPCT	PCT5.1	Valid N %

Example

```
/STATISTICS = COUNT (SEX (F7) STORE (F6) BUY).
```

- Two of the three variables have specific formats assigned for the COUNT function. The third variable takes the default format, F5.
- No explicit label is assigned to the COUNT function, so the default label *Count* appears under the value labels for each of the variables named.

Example

```
/STATISTICS = MEAN (OBS1 (COMMA9.2)).
```

- A COMMA format applies to the MEAN function for the variable *obs1*.
- No label is specified, so the default label *Mean* is used.

Example

```
/STATISTICS = SUM (OBS1 (DOLLAR10) '').
```

- A DOLLAR format applies to the sum of the variable *obs1*.
- A null label is specified for SUM.

STATISTICS: Percentage Bases

```
/STATISTICS = [{UNWEIGHTED}]
              {UNW      }
              {U        }
  {CPCT} [([varname] [({Fw.d        })] ['label']...[:base varlist])]
  {RPCT}             {PCTw.d       }
  {SPCT}             {PCTPARENw.d}
  {VPCT}
```

Example:

```
TABLES
        /TABLE = USINTL BY SEX > REGION
        /STATISTICS = CPCT (REGION (PCT4) '':SEX REGION).
```

		Respondent's Sex					
		Male			Female		
		Region of the United States			Region of the United States		
		North East	South East	West	North East	South East	West
Take Active Part in World Affairs	Active Part	78%	82%	82%	72%	70%	73%
	Stay Out	22%	18%	18%	28%	30%	28%

- A variable before the colon defines the numerator for calculating percentages.
- When multiple variables are named as numerators, a specified format and/or label apply only to the variable they follow.
- Variables after the colon (:base varlist) define a **base** (the denominator) for calculating percentages. This base applies to all variables specified for the function.

Overview

Four functions for calculating percentages are available with the STATISTICS subcommand. Each uses a different statistic as the numerator, and each has a different default for the base.

CPCT   *Count percentage.* The numerator is the cell count or, for group variables, a count of cases. The default base is the total number of cases in the table or, for group variables, the total number of cases or responses in the table (the GBASE subcommand specifies cases or responses). The default label is *Count (Dimension) %*. This function is valid for any variable.

CSPCT   *Case percentage.* The numerator is a count of cases. The default base is the total number of cases or responses depending upon the specified GBASE subcommand (see the GBASE subcommand). The default label is *Cases (Dimension) %*. This function is valid only for group variables and their totals.

RPCT   *Response percentage.* The numerator is the cell count of responses. The default base is the total number of cases or responses in the table, depending upon the specified GBASE subcommand (see the GBASE subcommand). The default label is *Responses (Dimension) %*. This function is valid only for group variables and their totals. The values shown for each category of the multiple-response variable are the same as those shown for case percentage; only the totals show different values.

SPCT   *Sum percentage.* The numerator is the cell sum. The default base is the sum for the table. The default label is *Sum (Dimension) %*. This function is valid only for totals and observation variables.

VPCT   *Valid* N *percentage.* The numerator is the valid cell count. The default base is the total number of valid cases in the table. The default label is *Valid N %*. This function is valid only for totals and observation variables.

For general information about the use of STATISTICS, see the STATISTICS subcommand. For information about the treatment of missing values for percentage numerators, see the MISSING subcommand. For information about missing values in the base, see the BASE subcommand.

Operations

- By default, a specified percentage function is calculated for each variable in the statistics dimension (see the STATISTICS subcommand) if the function is valid for the variable.
- The default format for percentages is PCT5.1.
- A percentage function uses weighted cases unless the function name is preceded by the keyword UNWEIGHTED (or U).

Bases and Percentage Types

Percentages are classified according to the table component that defines the base. **Table percentages** use the count or sum for a whole table as the base. The percentages for all the cells add to 100%. Table percentages for multiple stacked variables add to 100% across all the cells for each of the stacked variables. For example, six tables within the same display result when two variables are joined in the rows and three are joined in the columns. The percentages for each table add to 100%. See "Example" on p. 196.

If the percentage base is the count or sum for each column within a table, the percentages are **column percentages**, and they add to 100% within each column. Similarly, if the base is the count or sum for each row within a table, the percentages are **row percentages**, and they add to 100% within each row. When a TABLE subcommand specifies a nesting, the resulting table contains subtables, one for each value of the control variable. **Subtable percentages** use the count or sum for all the cells in a subtable as the base. (Separate layers are also referred to as subtables.)

The types of percentages that are produced depend on where the variables named on base variable lists are located in the table. Base variables displayed in the rows create row percentages. Base variables displayed in the columns create column percentages. Layer variables create percentages based on each layer of the table. Base variables that are control variables create subtable percentages. A percentage without an explicit base variable is a table percentage.

- The base variable list can name only category or group variables that are also named on the TABLE subcommand. This base applies to all variables specified for the function. Base has no effect on statistics other than percentages.
- If there is no base variable list, table percentages are produced.
- If the control variable for a nesting is specified as the base, subtable percentages are produced. If both the control variable and the nested variable are specified for the base, subtable, column, row, or layer percentages are produced according to the dimension of the nesting.
- If variables are stacked, you may include one or more of the stacked variables on the base variable list. Cells for stacked variables that are not on the base variable list use the default base rather than the specified base.
- To get percentages calculated on more than one base, specify multiple percentage functions with a different base for each.

Example

This example illustrates table, column, and row percentages.

```
TABLES
        /FTOTAL = T 'Total'
        /TABLE = SEX + T BY REGION + T
        /STATISTICS = COUNT(SEX'')
                      CPCT(SEX'Table %')
                      CPCT(SEX'Column %':REGION)
                      CPCT(SEX'Row %':SEX).
```

			Region of the United States			
			North East	South East	West	Total
Respondent's Sex	Male		281	177	178	636
		Table %	18.5%	11.7%	11.7%	41.9%
		Column %	41.4%	42.7%	42.1%	41.9%
		Row %	44.2%	27.8%	28.0%	100.0%
	Female		398	238	245	881
		Table %	26.2%	15.7%	16.2%	58.1%
		Column %	58.6%	57.3%	57.9%	58.1%
		Row %	45.2%	27.0%	27.8%	100.0%
Total			679	415	423	1517
	Table %		44.8%	27.4%	27.9%	100.0%
	Column %		100.0%	100.0%	100.0%	100.0%
	Row %		44.8%	27.4%	27.9%	100.0%

- Specifying the variable *sex* within parentheses for the first function, COUNT, causes rows to become the statistics dimension.

- No base variable is specified for the first CPCT function, so table percentages are produced by default. The appropriate label is assigned.
- For the second CPCT function, the column variable *region* is specified for the base. Accordingly, column percentages are produced.
- For the third CPCT function, the row variable *sex* is specified, producing row percentages.

Example

This example illustrates subtable percentages with nesting in the columns.

```
TABLES
      /FTOTAL = T 'Total'
      /TABLE = USINTL + T BY SEX > (REGION + T)
      /STATISTICS = COUNT(USINTL'')
                    CPCT(USINTL'Table %')
                    CPCT(USINTL'Subtable %':SEX).
```

			Respondent's Sex							
			Male				Female			
			Region of the United States				Region of the United States			
			North East	South East	West	**Total**	North East	South East	West	**Total**
Take Active Part in World Affairs	Active Part		138	94	102	**334**	189	113	116	**418**
		Table %	13.8%	9.4%	10.2%	**33.4%**	18.9%	11.3%	11.6%	**41.8%**
		Subtable %	33.1%	22.5%	24.5%	**80.1%**	32.5%	19.4%	19.9%	**71.8%**
	Stay Out		40	20	23	**83**	72	48	44	**164**
		Table %	4.0%	2.0%	2.3%	**8.3%**	7.2%	4.8%	4.4%	**16.4%**
		Subtable %	9.6%	4.8%	5.5%	**19.9%**	12.4%	8.2%	7.6%	**28.2%**
Total			178	114	125	**417**	261	161	160	**582**
	Table %		17.8%	11.4%	12.5%	**41.7%**	26.1%	16.1%	16.0%	**58.3%**
	Subtable %		42.7%	27.3%	30.0%	**100%**	44.8%	27.7%	27.5%	**100%**

- Because no base is specified on the first CPCT, table percentages are produced by default.
- The second CPCT function specifies the control variable *sex* as the base, so subtable percentages are produced.

Example

This example illustrates table, column, and row percentages with stacking.

```
TABLES
        /FTOTAL = T 'Total'
        /TABLE = USINTL + T BY REGION + T + SEX + T
        /STATISTICS = COUNT(USINTL'')
                      CPCT(USINTL'Table %')
                      CPCT(USINTL'Column %':REGION SEX)
                      CPCT(USINTL'Row %':USINTL).
```

			Region of the United States				Respondent's Sex		
			North East	South East	West	**Total**	Male	Female	**Total**
Take Active Part in World Affairs	Active Part		327	207	218	**752**	334	418	**752**
		Table %	32.7%	20.7%	21.8%	**75.3%**	33.4%	41.8%	**75.3%**
		Column %	74.5%	75.3%	76.5%	**75.3%**	80.1%	71.8%	**75.3%**
		Row %	43.5%	27.5%	29.0%	**100.0%**	44.4%	55.6%	**100.0%**
	Stay Out		112	68	67	**247**	83	164	**247**
		Table %	11.2%	6.8%	6.7%	**24.7%**	8.3%	16.4%	**24.7%**
		Column %	25.5%	24.7%	23.5%	**24.7%**	19.9%	28.2%	**24.7%**
		Row %	45.3%	27.5%	27.1%	**100.0%**	33.6%	66.4%	**100.0%**
Total			439	275	285	**999**	417	582	**999**
	Table %		**43.9%**	**27.5%**	**28.5%**	**100.0%**	**41.7%**	**58.3%**	**100.0%**
	Column %		**100.0%**	**100.0%**	**100.0%**	**100.0%**	**100.0%**	**100.0%**	**100.0%**
	Row %		**43.9%**	**27.5%**	**28.5%**	**100.0%**	**41.7%**	**58.3%**	**100.0%**

- Because the variable *region* is joined with the variable *sex*, there are two tables (*usintl* by *region* and *usintl* by *sex*) within the same display. Each table within the display adds up to 100% for table percentages.

- Because the second CPCT function specifies both *region* and *sex* on the base variable list, column percentages are produced for each table. (If only one variable were named, only columns for that variable would add up to 100%.)

- For the third CPCT function, the variable *usintl* is sufficient to produce row percentages for each table, because each row contains that variable.

Example

This example illustrates column percentages with nesting and stacking.

```
TABLES
  /FTOTAL = T 'Total'
  /TABLE = SEX > (USINTL + T + TAX + T) BY REGION + T
  /STATISTICS = CPCT(USINTL'' TAX'':REGION).
```

				Region of the United States			
				North East	South East	West	Total
Respondent's Sex	Male	Take Active Part in World Affairs	Active Part	31.4%	34.2%	35.8%	33.4%
			Stay Out	9.1%	7.3%	8.1%	8.3%
		Total		**40.5%**	**41.5%**	**43.9%**	**41.7%**
		R's Federal Income Tax	Too High	23.6%	27.0%	25.3%	25.0%
			About Right	20.0%	18.4%	17.8%	19.0%
			Too Low	.7%	.4%	.7%	.6%
		Total		**44.4%**	**45.9%**	**43.9%**	**44.6%**
	Female	Take Active Part in World Affairs	Active Part	43.1%	41.1%	40.7%	41.8%
			Stay Out	16.4%	17.5%	15.4%	16.4%
		Total		**59.5%**	**58.5%**	**56.1%**	**58.3%**
		R's Federal Income Tax	Too High	33.4%	31.1%	34.2%	33.0%
			About Right	22.0%	22.1%	21.2%	21.8%
			Too Low	.2%	.8%	.7%	.5%
		Total		**55.6%**	**54.1%**	**56.1%**	**55.4%**

- The variables *usintl* and *tax* are explicitly specified for the percentage, making rows the statistics dimension. (Remember that if a variable in a nesting is specified for statistics, it must be at the lowest level of nesting.)

- The variable *region* is named as the base for the percentage. Since *region* is the only variable in the columns, it produces column percentages. Notice that the totals for *usintl* add up to 100% in each column and that the totals for *tax* add up to 100% in each column.

- A null label is specified for the percentage. This forces the percentage to print in the same row as that of the category labels, which conserves space.

Percentage Types

There are four subtly different types of percentages: count, sum, response, and valid number percentages. For categorical variables, count percentages are always used. For observation variables, sum, count, or valid number percentages are used. For multiple-response variables, case and response percentages are used.

Count Percentage

CPCT gives counts as a percentage of the base.

- Category or group variables can be named as the base.
- The default format is PCT5.1, and the default label is *Count (Dimension) %*.
- If the CPCT function is applied to an observation variable, the function includes the missing values for that variable.
- CPCT applied to a multiple-response variable or to a total of a multiple-response variable uses the count of cases, not responses, as the numerator. This makes a difference only for the total of the multiple-response variable.
- With GBASE=CASES (the default), CPCT uses total cases as the denominator. With GBASE=RESPONSES, CPCT uses total responses as the denominator.

Case Percentage

CSPCT gives cases as a percentage of the base.

- CSPCT can be requested only for multiple-response variables or for totals of multiple-response variables.
- The default format is PCT5.1, and the default label is *Cases (Dimension) %*.
- CSPCT uses the count of cases, not responses, as the numerator. This makes a difference only for the total of the multiple-response variable.
- With GBASE=CASES (the default), CSPCT uses total cases as the denominator. With GBASE=RESPONSES, CSPCT uses total responses as the denominator.

Sum Percentage

SPCT gives the sum as a percentage of the base.

- SPCT can apply to an observation variable or to a total for a categorical or observation variable.
- The default format is PCT5.1, and the default label is *Sum (Dimension) %*.

Example

```
TABLES
      /OBSERVATION = CHILDS
      /FTOTAL = T 'Total'
      /TABLE = RACE > CHILDS + T BY REGION + T
      /STATISTICS = SUM('')
             SPCT('Table %')
             SPCT('Column %':REGION)
             SPCT('Row %':RACE).
```

				Region of the United States			
				North East	South East	West	Total
Race of Respondent	White	Number of Children		1086	558	660	2304
			Table %	37.9%	19.4%	23.0%	80.3%
			Column %	83.9%	70.1%	84.7%	80.3%
			Row %	47.1%	24.2%	28.6%	100.0%
	Black	Number of Children		185	209	63	457
			Table %	6.4%	7.3%	2.2%	15.9%
			Column %	14.3%	26.3%	8.1%	15.9%
			Row %	40.5%	45.7%	13.8%	100.0%
	Other	Number of Children		23	29	56	108
			Table %	.8%	1.0%	2.0%	3.8%
			Column %	1.8%	3.6%	7.2%	3.8%
			Row %	21.3%	26.9%	51.9%	100.0%
Total				1294	796	779	2869
	Table %			45.1%	27.7%	27.2%	100.0%
	Column %			100.0%	100.0%	100.0%	100.0%
	Row %			45.1%	27.7%	27.2%	100.0%

- SUM requests the cell sum.
- By default, SPCT shows table percentages.
- *Region* is in columns, so if *region* is named as the base, it produces column percentages.
- *Race* is in rows, so if *race* is named as the base, it produces row percentages. Note that because *childs* is an observation variable, it cannot be named as the base. Normally, a controlling variable (like *race*) used as a base produces subtable percentages. Because the variable nested under it is an observation variable and each subtable is a separate row, the base (*race*) produces row percentages (which, in this case, are the same as subtable percentages).

Response Percentage

RPCT gives responses as a percentage of the base. RPCT can be requested only for multiple-response variables or for totals of multiple-response variables.

- The default format is PCT5.1, and the default label is *Responses (Dimension) %*.
- With GBASE=CASES (the default), RPCT uses total cases as the denominator. With GBASE=RESPONSES, RPCT uses total responses as the denominator.

Example

The following TABLES command computes the percentage of cases using CPCT for a multiple-response variable.

```
TABLES
        /MRGROUP = PROB_C 'Most Significant Problems in the'+
        'Last 12 Months' PROB1 TO PROB4
        /FTOTAL = T 'Total'
        /TABLE = PROB_C + T BY SEX + T
        /STATISTICS = CASES(PROB_C'')
           CPCT(PROB_C'Table %')
           CPCT(PROB_C'Column %':SEX)
           CPCT(PROB_C'Row %':PROB_C).
```

			Respondent's Sex		
			Male	Female	Total
Most Significant Problems in the Last 12 Months	Health		48	90	138
		Table %	14.3%	26.8%	41.1%
		Column %	36.4%	44.1%	41.1%
		Row %	34.8%	65.2%	100.0%
	Finances		83	125	208
		Table %	24.7%	37.2%	61.9%
		Column %	62.9%	61.3%	61.9%
		Row %	39.9%	60.1%	100.0%
	Lack of Basic Services		4	3	7
		Table %	1.2%	.9%	2.1%
		Column %	3.0%	1.5%	2.1%
		Row %	57.1%	42.9%	100.0%
	Family		23	53	76
		Table %	6.8%	15.8%	22.6%
		Column %	17.4%	26.0%	22.6%
		Row %	30.3%	69.7%	100.0%
	Personal		15	26	41
		Table %	4.5%	7.7%	12.2%
		Column %	11.4%	12.7%	12.2%
		Row %	36.6%	63.4%	100.0%
	Legal		1	1	2
		Table %	.3%	.3%	.6%
		Column %	.8%	.5%	.6%
		Row %	50.0%	50.0%	100.0%
	Miscellaneous		23	48	71
		Table %	6.8%	14.3%	21.1%
		Column %	17.4%	23.5%	21.1%
		Row %	32.4%	67.6%	100.0%
Total			132	204	336
	Table %		39.3%	60.7%	100.0%
	Column %		100.0%	100.0%	100.0%
	Row %		39.3%	60.7%	100.0%

- The total counts for the table and the columns are less than the sums of the respective statistics in the cells, because *prob_c* is a multiple-response variable and CASES has been specified as the counting function.

- Because GBASE=CASES is the default, the total cases are used for the percentage bases. Note that total column percentages and table percentages are each 100%.

- Row variables add up as you would expect them to, because *sex* is a normal category variable.

Example

The following TABLES command computes the percentage of responses using RPCT for the same multiple-response variable.

```
TABLES
        /MRGROUP = PROB_C 'Most Significant Problems in the'+
        'Last 12 Months' PROB1 TO PROB4
        /GBASE = RESPONSES
        /FTOTAL = T 'Total'
        /TABLE = PROB_C + T BY SEX + T
        /STATISTICS = RESPONSES(PROB_C'')
                    RPCT(PROB_C'Table %')
                    RPCT(PROB_C'Column %':SEX)
                    RPCT(PROB_C'Row %':PROB_C).
```

| | | | Respondent's Sex | | Total |
			Male	Female	
Most Significant Problems in the Last 12 Months	Health		48	90	138
		Table %	8.8%	16.6%	25.4%
		Column %	24.4%	26.0%	25.4%
		Row %	34.8%	65.2%	100.0%
	Finances		83	125	208
		Table %	15.3%	23.0%	38.3%
		Column %	42.1%	36.1%	38.3%
		Row %	39.9%	60.1%	100.0%
	Lack of Basic Services		4	3	7
		Table %	.7%	.6%	1.3%
		Column %	2.0%	.9%	1.3%
		Row %	57.1%	42.9%	100.0%
	Family		23	53	76
		Table %	4.2%	9.8%	14.0%
		Column %	11.7%	15.3%	14.0%
		Row %	30.3%	69.7%	100.0%
	Personal		15	26	41
		Table %	2.8%	4.8%	7.6%
		Column %	7.6%	7.5%	7.6%
		Row %	36.6%	63.4%	100.0%
	Legal		1	1	2
		Table %	.2%	.2%	.4%
		Column %	.5%	.3%	.4%
		Row %	50.0%	50.0%	100.0%
	Miscellaneous		23	48	71
		Table %	4.2%	8.8%	13.1%
		Column %	11.7%	13.9%	13.1%
		Row %	32.4%	67.6%	100.0%
Total			197	346	543
	Table %		36.3%	63.7%	100.0%
	Column %		100.0%	100.0%	100.0%
	Row %		36.3%	63.7%	100.0%

- The GBASE subcommand requests responses, not counts, for the percentage base.
- The RESPONSES function on the STATISTICS subcommand shows the number of responses in each cell.
- RPCT shows the percentage of responses in each cell.
- Now the totals for table percentages and column percentages are equal to the sums of the respective statistics in the cells. Since GBASE=RESPONSES was specified, total column and table percentages are 100%.

Valid N Percentage

VPCT gives the valid number of cases as a percentage of the base.

- VPCT is valid only for observation variables.
- VPCT gives results identical to those of CPCT, except that missing cases are not included in the count.
- The default format is PCT5.1, and the default label is *Valid N %*.

TABLE

```
/TABLE = rows [BY columns [BY layers ]]
```

Example:

```
TABLES
        /TABLE = USINTL BY REGION BY SEX.
```

Respondent's Sex Male

		Region of the United States		
		North East	South East	West
Take Active Part in World Affairs	Active Part	138	94	102
	Stay Out	40	20	23

Respondent's Sex Female

		Region of the United States		
		North East	South East	West
Take Active Part in World Affairs	Active Part	189	113	116
	Stay Out	72	48	44

- The TABLE subcommand is the first local subcommand after all the global subcommands. Any number of TABLE subcommands can be used. For each one, any other local subcommands that apply to it must come immediately after the TABLE subcommand.
- The row expression on the TABLE subcommand must precede the optional column expression, and both must precede the optional layer expression. The keyword BY must separate one expression from another.
- Expressions are constructed from working data file variables, group variables, totals, and the keywords (LABELS) and (STATISTICS). When more than one of these elements are specified for one dimension, they are separated by + and/or > operators. The + operator stacks variables one above the other. The > operator nests the variable following it beneath the variable preceding it. Parentheses control the order of the operations.
- Before the first TABLE subcommand, the subcommands OBSERVATION, MDGROUP or MRGROUP, and FTOTAL or PTOTAL must be used to declare any observation variables, multiple-response variables, and totals.

Overview

TABLE is a local subcommand, the only one required in the procedure. The TABLE subcommand defines a table's structure. A table can have one, two, or three dimensions, each defined by a single variable or by an expression that combines multiple variables in the same dimension.

Two keywords can be specified on TABLE:

(LABELS)   *Prints a dimension with value labels only and, optionally, totals.*

(STATISTICS)   *Moves the statistics to another dimension.*

These keywords are discussed below. Note that the parentheses are part of the specification.

Operations

- One row, column, or layer is created for each statistic requested.
- Empty rows and columns are retained only when a value exists for a row or column variable in one layer but not in another. This may also occur with stacked variables when a variable is present in one stacked variable in a row or column but not the other.
- Only the row dimension can be requested without other dimensions.
- By default, variables from the working data file are treated as category variables.

Multivariable Dimensions

Stacking and nesting combine items within a single dimension on a TABLE subcommand. In this context, the term "item" refers to a variable or a combination of variables. Each stacking or nesting combines two items at a time, although more than one operator can appear within the same dimension.

Stacking

The + sign stacks an item in the same dimension as the item before the + sign. This produces a display in which the combined items simply appear next to each other along one dimension. Otherwise, the two items have no direct connection or effect on each other. For example, when one item is stacked with another in the column dimension, the typical result is a single display with two tables that have common row titles but different column titles. The two tables are stacked along the horizontal dimension, as if completely separate tables had simply been pasted together. If table percentages are computed, the base for the percentages is defined by the counts or sums for the individual tables rather than by the count or sum for the whole display (see "STATISTICS: Percentage Bases" on p. 192).

TABLE   207

Example

```
TABLES
        /TABLE = USINTL + TAX BY SEX + RACE.
```

		Respondent's Sex		Race of Respondent		
		Male	Female	White	Black	Other
Take Active Part in World Affairs	Active Part	334	418	654	78	20
	Stay Out	83	164	194	47	6
R's Federal Income Tax	Too High	233	308	445	71	25
	About Right	177	203	332	37	11
	Too Low	6	5	11		

- Stacking occurs in both dimensions. *Usintl* and *tax* are stacked in the rows, and *sex* and *race* are stacked in the columns.
- Effectively, four different tables are displayed together: *usintl* by *sex*, *tax* by *sex*, *usintl* by *race*, and *tax* by *race*.

Nesting

The > sign nests an item beneath the preceding item. An item preceding the > sign is a **control item**, and an item following the operator is a **nested item**. All the values of the nested item are tabulated within each value of the control item. The effect is the same as a crosstabulation, although nesting "crosstabulates" in a single dimension. Individual values of the control item define different **subtables**.

- Multiple levels of nesting are permitted.
- An observation variable cannot nest within another observation variable. The expressions OBS1 > OBS2 and (OBS1 + VAR2) > OBS2 are both illegal (see "Observation Variables" on p. 211).
- A total cannot nest within another total, and a total cannot be applied to a nesting that includes a total. The expressions (VAR1 + FTOT) > (VAR2 + FTOT) and PTOT + VAR1 > (VAR2 + FTOT) are both illegal (see "Totals" on p. 216).

Example

```
/TABLE = USINTL > TAX BY SEX > RACE.
```

				Respondent's Sex					
				Male			Female		
				Race of Respondent			Race of Respondent		
				White	Black	Other	White	Black	Other
Take Active Part in World Affairs	Active Part	R's Federal Income Tax	Too High	88	5	4	86	13	6
			About Right	60	9		71	4	1
			Too Low	3			2		
	Stay Out	R's Federal Income Tax	Too High	22	2	1	32	12	1
			About Right	12	2	1	22	3	1
			Too Low				1		

- Nesting occurs in both dimensions.
- Each nesting is crosstabulated with the other nesting, creating four subtables within one table.
- The TABLE subcommand in this example has nesting operators in place of the stacking operators in the previous example. A key difference between the resulting tables is that the variables in each dimension of the nested table are in effect crosstabulated, whereas the variables in each dimension of the stacked table remain separate.

Order of Operations

Normally, nesting is performed before stacking.

Example

```
/TABLE = SEX > USINTL + TAX BY REGION.
```

| | | | | Region of the United States | | |
				North East	South East	West
Respondent's Sex	Male	Take Active Part in World Affairs	Active Part	138	94	102
			Stay Out	40	20	23
	Female	Take Active Part in World Affairs	Active Part	189	113	116
			Stay Out	72	48	44
R's Federal Income Tax	Too High			239	142	160
	About Right			176	99	105
	Too Low			4	3	4

- In the row expression, *usintl* is nested within *sex*, and *tax* is stacked with the nested variables. *Tax* is not nested within *sex*.

TABLE   209

Changed Order of Operations

You can change the normal order of operations by using parentheses. An expression within parentheses is evaluated first.

Example

```
/TABLE = SEX > (USINTL + TAX) BY REGION.
```

				Region of the United States		
				North East	South East	West
Respondent's Sex	Male	Take Active Part in World Affairs	Active Part	138	94	102
			Stay Out	40	20	23
		R's Federal Income Tax	Too High	99	66	68
			About Right	84	45	48
			Too Low	3	1	2
	Female	Take Active Part in World Affairs	Active Part	189	113	116
			Stay Out	72	48	44
		R's Federal Income Tax	Too High	140	76	92
			About Right	92	54	57
			Too Low	1	2	2

- In the row expression, *usintl* is stacked with *tax*, and both are nested under *sex*.

Example

```
/TABLE = SEX + USINTL > TAX BY REGION.
```

				Region of the United States		
				North East	South East	West
Respondent's Sex	Male			281	177	178
	Female			398	238	245
Take Active Part in World Affairs	Active Part	R's Federal Income Tax	Too High	91	56	55
			About Right	61	39	45
			Too Low	2	1	2
	Stay Out	R's Federal Income Tax	Too High	30	20	20
			About Right	17	7	17
			Too Low		1	

- Nesting occurs before stacking. Thus, *tax* is nested under *usintl*, which is stacked with *sex*. *Tax* is not nested under *sex*.

Example

```
/TABLE = (SEX + USINTL) > TAX BY REGION.
```

				Region of the United States		
				North East	South East	West
Respondent's Sex	Male	R's Federal Income Tax	Too High	99	66	68
			About Right	84	45	48
			Too Low	3	1	2
	Female	R's Federal Income Tax	Too High	140	76	92
			About Right	92	54	57
			Too Low	1	2	2
Take Active Part in World Affairs	Active Part	R's Federal Income Tax	Too High	91	56	55
			About Right	61	39	45
			Too Low	2	1	2
	Stay Out	R's Federal Income Tax	Too High	30	20	20
			About Right	17	7	17
			Too Low		1	

- Expressions within parentheses are evaluated first. Thus, *tax* is nested under *sex* and *usintl*, which are stacked below each other.

Category Variables

Variables named on the TABLE subcommand that come from the working data file are assumed to be category variables, unless specifically declared otherwise. The Tables procedure creates a row, column, or layer for each value of a category variable (or for each combination of the values in a nesting).

- Multiple-response variables created on the MDGROUP or MRGROUP subcommand follow the same rules as category variables.
- Category variables can have alphanumeric values, but the values are truncated to the limit set for short strings.

Limitations

- The Tables procedure allows a maximum of 100 category variables.
- There is no limit on the number of unique values in a category variable.
- To limit the range for a category variable, select cases with the transformation language before using the Tables procedure.

TABLE   211

Observation Variables

Observation variables must be declared on the OBSERVATION subcommand before being named on the TABLE subcommand.

- All observation variables come from the working data file and must be numeric.
- All observation variables in a table must be specified for the same dimension.
- Separate summary statistics requested for an observation variable in the rows, columns, or layers dimension produce separate rows, columns, or layers, respectively.

Example

```
TABLES
      /OBSERVATION = AGE EDUC
      /TABLE = SEX BY AGE + EDUC
      /STATISTICS = MEDIAN MODE.
```

		Age of Respondent		Highest Year of School Completed	
		Median	Mode	Median	Mode
Respondent's Sex	Male	41	35	13	12
	Female	42	35	12	12

- The observation variables are in the columns dimension.
- Two summary statistics (MEDIAN and MODE) are requested, producing two columns for each observation variable.

Nesting Observation Variables

Observation variables may be nested within a category variable, or a category variable may be nested within an observation variable.

- An observation variable cannot nest within another observation variable. The following two expressions are both illegal:

```
OBS1 > OBS2
(OBS1 + VAR2) > OBS2
```

- If an observation variable is nested within a category or group variable, the order of nesting does not affect the numbers produced or the structure of the table; it affects only the labeling. Regardless of how the nesting was specified, the Tables procedure creates a row, column, or layer for each observation statistic.
- If a category or group variable is specified as nested within an observation variable, a label for the observation variable precedes the category or group variable in the display.
- If an observation variable is specified as nested within a category or group variable, a label for the observation variable follows each value label for the category or group variable.

Example

```
TABLES
    /OBSERVATION = AGE
    /TABLE = REGION BY AGE > SEX
    /TABLE = REGION BY SEX > AGE.
```

		Age of Respondent	
		Respondent's Sex	
		Male	Female
Region of the United States	North East	44	47
	South East	46	49
	West	43	44

		Respondent's Sex	
		Male	Female
		Age of Respondent	Age of Respondent
Region of the United States	North East	44	47
	South East	46	49
	West	43	44

- The observation variable is in the columns.
- On the first TABLE subcommand, *sex* is nested within *age*.
- On the second TABLE subcommand, *age* is nested within *sex*.
- Both tables show the same statistics, but the column titles are organized differently.

Creating a Labels Dimension

Use the keyword (LABELS) on the TABLE subcommand to create a table with the value labels in one dimension and variables in another dimension. The keyword is placed on a TABLE subcommand as if it were a variable. Note that the parentheses are part of the keyword. (LABELS) has the following capabilities and restrictions:

- Only category variables can be used with the (LABELS) keyword. Multiple-response variables, totals, and the (STATISTICS) keyword are illegal in the dimension from which (LABELS) takes the variable labels. Observation variables may be used only in this dimension if they are nested within a category variable. Observation variables in this dimension may not be stacked with category variables (but may be stacked with other observation variables).
- If multiple variables are used, they should all have the same value labels.

TABLE   213

- (LABELS) can be used only once on a TABLE subcommand.
- (LABELS) cannot be used in the layer dimension.
- (LABELS) can be stacked only with PTOTAL and FTOTAL variables.
- (LABELS) may be nested within category or observation variables. The (STATISTICS) keyword may be nested within the (LABELS) keyword.
- Explicit statistics can apply only to variables, not (LABELS).
- When the STATISTICS subcommand is used and multiple statistics are requested, the statistics labels are placed in the same dimension as each variable label, not each value label. If you want to nest statistics within the value labels, nest the (STATISTICS) keyword within the (LABELS) keyword.
- The default statistic with the (LABELS) option is COUNT.

Example

```
TABLES
     /TABLE=OBEY+POPULAR+THNKSELF BY (LABELS).
```

	Most Important	2nd Important	3rd Important	4th Important	Least Important
To Obey	195	123	142	343	179
To Be Well Liked or Popular	4	27	57	185	709
To Think for Oneself	510	161	130	135	46

- The row variables all have the same value labels.
- Each value is shown as a separate column. Each variable is a separate row.

Example

```
TABLES
     /TABLE=OBEY+POPULAR+THNKSELF BY SEX > (LABELS).
```

	Respondent's Sex									
	Male					Female				
	Most Important	2nd Important	3rd Important	4th Important	Least Important	Most Important	2nd Important	3rd Important	4th Important	Least Important
To Obey	87	53	62	123	83	108	70	80	220	96
To Be Well Liked or Popular	2	15	33	83	275	2	12	24	102	434
To Think for Oneself	193	79	52	61	23	317	82	78	74	23

- Again, the row variables all have the same value labels.
- Each value of the row variables is a column nested under *sex*.
- The FORMAT subcommand makes the columns narrower, so the table fits on the page.

Creating a Statistics Dimension

Use the (STATISTICS) keyword with the TABLE subcommand to create a table with statistics in a separate dimension. Like (LABELS), (STATISTICS) is placed on a TABLE subcommand as if it were a variable. Again, the parentheses are part of the keyword. The (STATISTICS) keyword has capabilities and restrictions similar to those of (LABELS).

- (STATISTICS) can be used in any dimension.
- (STATISTICS) can be stacked only with PTOTAL and FTOTAL variables. If (STATISTICS) is nested beneath a variable, that group may be stacked with another group composed of a variable with (STATISTICS) nested beneath.
- (STATISTICS) can be nested beneath observation and category variables and the (LABELS) keyword. (STATISTICS) cannot be nested beneath a total or multiple-response set.
- (STATISTICS) must be at the lowest level of nesting.
- All variables in the statistics dimension should be assigned the same statistics. If they are not, the (STATISTICS) keyword cannot be applied correctly. In this case, the statistics will be taken from the first (nontotal) variable and a warning will be issued.
- Unlike (LABELS), (STATISTICS) may be used more than once. However, all instances of the (STATISTICS) keyword must be in the same dimension. If (STATISTICS) occurs more than once, each instance must be nested beneath variables that are concatenated.

Example

```
TABLES
    /TABLE=OBEY+POPULAR+THNKSELF BY (STATISTICS)
    /STATISTICS=COUNT CPCT.
```

		Count	Count Percent
To Obey	Most Important	195	19.9%
	2nd Important	123	12.5%
	3rd Important	142	14.5%
	4th Important	343	34.9%
	Least Important	179	18.2%
To Be Well Liked or Popular	Most Important	4	.4%
	2nd Important	27	2.7%
	3rd Important	57	5.8%
	4th Important	185	18.8%
	Least Important	709	72.2%
To Think for Oneself	Most Important	510	51.9%
	2nd Important	161	16.4%
	3rd Important	130	13.2%
	4th Important	135	13.7%
	Least Important	46	4.7%

TABLE   215

- The row variables are all assigned the same statistics.
- Each statistic is shown as a separate column. Each variable label is a separate row.

Example

```
TABLES
    /TABLE=OBEY+POPULAR+THNKSELF BY SEX > (STATISTICS)
    /STATISTICS=COUNT CPCT.
```

| | | Respondent's Sex | | | |
| | | Male | | Female | |
		Count	Count Percent	Count	Count Percent
To Obey	Most Important	87	8.9%	108	11.0%
	2nd Important	53	5.4%	70	7.1%
	3rd Important	62	6.3%	80	8.1%
	4th Important	123	12.5%	220	22.4%
	Least Important	83	8.5%	96	9.8%
To Be Well Liked or Popular	Most Important	2	.2%	2	.2%
	2nd Important	15	1.5%	12	1.2%
	3rd Important	33	3.4%	24	2.4%
	4th Important	83	8.5%	102	10.4%
	Least Important	275	28.0%	434	44.2%
To Think for Oneself	Most Important	193	19.7%	317	32.3%
	2nd Important	79	8.0%	82	8.4%
	3rd Important	52	5.3%	78	7.9%
	4th Important	61	6.2%	74	7.5%
	Least Important	23	2.3%	23	2.3%

- Again, the row variables all have the same statistics.
- Each statistic for the row variables is a column nested under *sex*.

Example

```
TABLES
 /FTOTAL=TOTAL
 /TABLE=THNKSELF BY RACE>(STATISTICS)+SEX>(STATISTICS)+TOTAL
 /STATISTICS=CPCT.
```

		Race of Respondent			Respondent's Sex		**TOTAL**
		White	Black	Other	Male	Female	
		Count Percent	Count Percent	Count Percent	Count Percent	Count Percent	**Count Percent**
To Think for Oneself	Most Important	45.8%	5.3%	.8%	19.7%	32.3%	**51.9%**
	2nd Important	13.3%	2.4%	.6%	8.0%	8.4%	**16.4%**
	3rd Important	10.3%	2.3%	.6%	5.3%	7.9%	**13.2%**
	4th Important	10.3%	2.7%	.7%	6.2%	7.5%	**13.7%**
	Least Important	3.5%	.9%	.3%	2.3%	2.3%	**4.7%**

- This is an alternative to the syntax:

```
TABLES
 /FTOTAL=TOTAL
 /TABLE=THNKSELF BY RACE+SEX+TOTAL
 /STATISTICS=CPCT(RACE) CPCT(SEX).
```

Both produce the same table.

Totals

Totals must be defined on a TOTALS subcommand before they can be used on the TABLE subcommand.

- A total reserves a row, column, or layer for summary statistics.
- A total is stacked with the item it summarizes. A following total (defined on FTOTAL) must follow a stacking operator on the TABLE subcommand. A preceding total (defined on PTOTAL) must precede a stacking operator. A TABLE specification, such as the following example, clarifies the distinction between FTOTAL and PTOTAL:

```
/TABLE = VAR1 + TOTAL + VAR2
```

Here, if the total is a following total, it totals *var1*. If the total is a preceding total, it totals *var2*.

- In a table display, the row, column, or layer reserved by a following total follows the item that the total summarizes. Similarly, a preceding total precedes its summarized item.
- Totals specified for the rows produce rows that contain column summary statistics. Totals for the columns produce columns containing row summaries. Totals for the layer dimension produce layers containing layer summaries.

TABLE   217

- An item that is summarized cannot include another total. The following expression is illegal because it calls for an FTOTAL to summarize a PTOTAL:

```
VAR1 > (PTOT + VAR3) + FTOT
```

Example

```
TABLES
        /OBSERVATION = age
        /FTOTAL = FTOT 'Following total'
        /PTOTAL = PTOT 'Preceding total'
        /TABLE = REGION > USINTL + FTOT BY PTOT + AGE > SEX
        /STATISTICS = RANGE.
```

				Preceding total	Age of Respondent	
					Respondent's Sex	
					Male	Female
				Range	Range	Range
Region of the United States	North East	Take Active Part in World Affairs	Active Part	68	62	68
			Stay Out	70	67	70
	South East	Take Active Part in World Affairs	Active Part	65	61	65
			Stay Out	61	55	61
	West	Take Active Part in World Affairs	Active Part	69	62	69
			Stay Out	67	67	62
Following total				71	69	70

- Each of the two totals summarizes a nesting.
- Where the total row and the total column cross, the statistic summarizes the whole table.

Totals and Adjacent Symbols

On a TABLE subcommand, only certain symbols are valid at the immediate left or right of a following or preceding total. The eligible symbols for each total are:

```
    ...+   ftotal { BY }
                  { )  }
                  { +  }
                  { /  }

    { =  } ptotal  +...
    { BY }
    { (  }
    { +  }
```

For *following* totals, the valid symbols are used in these ways:

+   When the stack operator is to the *left* of a following total, the operator links the total to the item it summarizes. The total shown below summarizes everything before it:

```
VAR3 > (VAR1 + VAR2) + FTOT
```

When the stack operator is to the *right* of a following total, the operator places the total before the next item. The total does not summarize the next item or have any other effect on it. Here, the total summarizes *var1*.

```
VAR1 + FTOT + (VAR3 + VAR4) > VAR2
```

BY This keyword appears to the right of a following total to separate the total from the next dimension (the columns or layers dimension).

) The right parenthesis appears to the right of a following total when the total is stacked after a variable that is nested within another item. Here, the total summarizes *var3>var2* and then *var1>var2*.

```
(VAR3 + VAR1) > (VAR2 + FTOT)
```

/ The terminator for a TABLE subcommand appears to the right of a following total if the total is the last item named on the subcommand.

For *preceding* totals, the valid adjacent symbols are used in these ways:

+ When the stack operator is to the *right* of a preceding total, the operator links the total to the item it summarizes. For example, the total shown below summarizes everything after it:

```
PTOT + VAR3 > (VAR1 + VAR2)
```

When the stack operator is to the *left* of a preceding total, the operator joins the total after the prior item. The total does not summarize the prior item or have any other effect on it.

```
VAR3 > VAR1 + PTOT + VAR2
```

= An equals sign to the left of a preceding total means that the total is the first item named on the TABLE subcommand. For example, the total summarizes *var1>var2*.

```
/TABLE = PTOT + VAR1 > VAR2 BY VAR3
```

BY This keyword appears to the left of a preceding total to separate the total from the prior dimension (the rows or columns dimension).

(The left parenthesis appears to the left of a preceding total when the total is stacked before an item that is nested within another item. For example, the total summarizes *var3>var2* and *var1>var2*.

```
(VAR3 + VAR1) > (PTOT + VAR2)
```

A nesting operator cannot come before or after a total because a total cannot be included directly in a nesting. However, a total can be nested indirectly within another item if the total is part of a stacked item. For example, these expressions are valid:

```
VAR1 > (VAR2 + FTOT)
VAR1 > (PTOT + VAR2)
```

Subject Index

Syntax Index